Understanding and Trans
ATTENTION-SEEKING BEHAVI(

JORDAN R. CHAVEZ IV, M.D.

The Mindset Media

Jordan R. Chavez IV, M.D.

Understanding and Transforming
ATTENTION-SEEKING BEHAVIORS in CHILDREN

Author
Dr. Jordan R. Chavez IV

Copyright © [2024] by Dr. Jordan R. Chavez IV
All rights reserved.

No part of this book may be reproduced, distributed, or transmitted in any form or by any means, including photocopying, recording, or other electronic or mechanical methods, without the prior written permission of the author, except in the case of brief quotations embodied in critical articles and reviews.

Printed in the Philippines

Cover Design by
Dr. Jordan R. Chavez IV

To all the parents who tirelessly navigate the beautiful chaos of raising children, this book is dedicated to you. Your unwavering love, patience, and resilience shape the hearts and minds of the next generation. May you find comfort, inspiration, and practical wisdom within these pages to help you understand and transform the attention-seeking behaviors of your children into opportunities for deeper connection and growth. Remember, you are not alone on this journey. Your efforts, no matter how small they may seem, are the building blocks of a brighter future for your children. Thank you for your endless dedication and for being the guiding light in your child's life.

Jordan R. Chavez IV, M.D.

Table of Contents

Table of Contents 4
Preface 6
Chapter 1 10
   Introduction to Attention-Seeking Behaviors 10
Chapter 2 17
   Childhood Development and the Roots of Attention-Seeking ... 17
Chapter 3 25
   Environmental Factors Contributing to Attention-Seeking 25
Chapter 4 34
   The Different Types of Attention-Seeking Behaviors in Early Childhood 34
Chapter 5 42
   The Emotional Drivers Behind Attention-Seeking 42
Chapter 6 51
   The Role of Parenting Styles in Attention-Seeking 51
Chapter 7 61
   Attention-Seeking Behaviors in Adolescence 61
Chapter 9 79
   How to React to Attention-Seeking Behavior (Short-Term Strategies) 79
Chapter 11 95
   Encouraging Healthy Attention-Seeking Through Positive Reinforcement 95
Chapter 12 103
   Teaching Children Self-Sufficiency and Confidence 103
Chapter 13 111
   The Role of Educators and School Environments in Addressing Attention-Seeking 111
Chapter 14 120
   Parental Self-Care and Emotional Balance 120
Chapter 15 128

Transforming Attention-Seeking into Constructive and Trusting Relationships 128
Conclusion *136*
A Framework for Lifelong Empowerment 136
Epilogue *144*
About the Author *149*

Jordan R. Chavez IV, M.D.

Preface

I have been a doctor for 24 years, with eighteen of those years spent as a pediatrician in the emergency room. I am also the father of five fabulous kids named Lia, Ethan, Elai, Maya, and Josh. When I think about my life, one theme keeps coming up: the many ways kids try to get your attention. In my job, I have met a lot of families whose lives are messed up by habits they call "attention-seeking." These families are often frustrated and do not know where to get help. I have been through these things in my personal life, and even though I am a parent with years of medical experience, I sometimes feel just as lost.

One of the most rewarding and humbling things I have ever done was raise five kids, each with their own style and temperament. It can be hard for parents to figure out what their kids need emotionally while juggling everyday life's pressures. I have learned that any behavior that is done to get attention hides a much deeper need: the need to connect. This is true for both my oldest daughter, Lia, who was very independent when she was young, and my youngest son, Josh, who always needed reassurance before taking on new challenges.

ATTENTION-SEEKING BEHAVIORS in CHILDREN

That link, along with the successes and failures of parenting, as well as the hundreds of families I have helped as a doctor, led to the writing of this book. Most of the time, when parents take their kids to the emergency room, the talk starts with a physical symptom and quickly turns to worries about behavior problems. Not only are these parents looking for medical answers, but they are also looking for ways to get back in touch with their children in the middle of the chaos of daily life. I came to the realization that the word "attention-seeking" was not the right one. It is often taken in a bad way like the child's needs are not important. But the truth is that every time a child tries to get your attention, it is a clear and true call for connection, love, validation, and affirmation.

During my career, I have seen and experienced a wide range of attention-seeking behaviors, from toddlers throwing temper tantrums when they feel ignored to teens who, through silence or defiance, are just trying to be seen as they navigate the more complicated stages of becoming an adult. More importantly, I have seen and lived through the huge changes that can happen when parents react with understanding and empathy instead of anger or frustration.

This book gives you a way to look at attention-seeking behaviors not as "bad" behavior but as a child's way of expressing an emotional need. It is a kind way to raise kids in a world where parents feel like they need to know everything. It supports self-reflection, emotional connection, and growth for everyone. It is my hope that this book will help parents, caregivers, teachers, and even medical workers make the deeper connections that are necessary to understand and meet a child's basic emotional needs.

There are tips in this book that will help you do the following:

- Think of behavior trying to get attention as a good and regular part of growing up emotionally.

- Find out how to balance the need for care with teaching kids to be independent.
- Help kids say what they need more helpfully to feel seen, heard, and respected.
- Figure out the patterns in how you respond that either make things worse or better.
- Make sure your child feels safe, loved, and connected. This will help both of you for the rest of your lives.

I clearly remember when my second child, Ethan, was about seven years old and could not wait to show his brothers his latest school project. He begged me to pay attention, but I was busy and fought the urge to just rest after a long shift in the emergency room. These little moments, which happen repeatedly in many homes worldwide, tell me that kids do not just want attention for the sake of attention. They want to feel important to their parents by being heard. By focusing on Ethan, I not only made him feel seen, but I also grew as a person, even though I was exhausted at the time.

In this book, I will tell Lia, Ethan, Elai, Maya, and Josh my stories and the stories of patients and families I have enjoyed working with. I hope that these stories will make you think of your family problems and remind you that every child will go through times when they test their limits, ask for more than they think they can give, and show feelings that are hard to handle. But these times are also chances, which I know because I have learned it as a pediatrician and a parent of five kids.

As a dad, I can tell you that being a parent is always a process of learning. As a doctor, I can tell you that you are not the only one going through these things. Families all over the world have the same problems. However, there is a chance for an even greater connection in all these things. That link, which can be grown through patience, understanding, and interest, is the key to turning attention-seeking behaviors into a way to grow, build trust, and feel emotionally intense.

ATTENTION-SEEKING BEHAVIORS in CHILDREN

If you are a parent or caretaker who picks up this book, I hope you find both practical information and comforting words inside. I hope you find, as I have on my own path, that attention-seeking habits are not a sign of failure on the part of either the child or the parent but rather a chance to get closer and strengthen your bond. Sometimes, your child will try to get your attention, but I hope you can see this as an opportunity to show them that they are and always will be the most important person in your life.

Thank you for letting me be a part of your journey as a parent. Let us keep making our kids emotionally safe, confident, and connected one moment, one talk, and one shared experience at a time.

With gratitude and hope,

JORDAN R. CHAVEZ IV
Pediatrician, Father, and Student of Life

Jordan R. Chavez IV, M.D.

Chapter 1

Introduction to Attention-Seeking Behaviors

As a father of five and a pediatrician with almost twenty years of experience, I have personally seen the many attention-seeking behaviors that kids, both my own and my patients, show. These actions can be harmless or annoying, but they all have one thing in common: a deep-seated need to be seen, heard, and accepted. Attention, or the lack of it, can have a significant impact on who a child becomes during their growing years. This has been true for me whether I was in a busy emergency room or a quiet house with my own kids.

Let me take you back to a night in the emergency room. A woman walks in with her five-year-old son Keith. Keith was not extremely sick; he had a small fever and some light cold symptoms. But it was not his sickness that stood out; it was how he behaved. Keith kept grabbing his mom's phone and pulling on her coat, loudly cutting us off from any talk we were trying to have. It was clear from the look of despair in his eyes. The scene made me think of my son Ethan when he was about the same age. Ethan, who was active and full of life, had his way of getting my attention. He would often insist on talking over his older sister Lia at dinner when she was trying to talk about her day.

They were both doing things that psychologists call "attention-seeking" behavior. Ethan and Keith were not being hard to have a good relationship with just because they could. Instead, they wanted to be noticed and felt like they were being seen, heard, and cared for. Their behavior made me think of something basic that I had seen a lot of times at work and at home: wanting attention is neither a fault nor a flaw. For kids, it is a sign that they need to connect with others.

What attention-seeking behaviors are and how they work

You can break down attention-seeking habits into the things a child (or adult) does or says to get the attention of the people around them. Some people might get the wrong idea and think these acts are only meant to trick or cause trouble. It is understandable why parents might get angry when their kids act out like that, but attention-seeking is not inherently bad. According to evolutionary theory, wanting attention from caregivers is an effective way to stay alive (Bowlby, 1969).

To return to Keith's case, his frequent interruptions and defiant actions toward his mother were not random. One could say that his actions came from the biological need to be noticed and liked. Like Ethan talking over Lia, Keith's main way of communicating was to get attention. It was my job to tell his mother that this behavior was more about wanting to connect with others than anything else.

When we consider what attention-seeking really means, we should distinguish healthy forms, like a child showing off a drawing to get praise, from dangerous extremes, like acting out, throwing fits, or being physically violent all the time. The less severe forms do not usually cause much trouble, but the more severe ones can hurt relationships well into adulthood if they are ignored or treated badly.

According to Dr. Gwen Dewar (2013), these behaviors are a normal part of growing up for young children and help them learn how to benefit from adult care, advice, and attention. They also help them learn how to act in social situations and say what they need, whether it is something physical or mental.

Attention and How It Helps Children Grow

Lia was not the only one who tried to get Ethan's attention as he got older. Soon, his younger brother Elai joined the fight, which made our dinner talks full of interruptions and angry outbursts. I remember how hard it was to balance my time with a busy ER schedule and a growing family. It was during those years that I really started to understand how important care is for a child's growth.

Kids naturally want to interact with the world around them, and how they get that interaction back affects a lot of their growth. When a kid yells, "Look at me!" or "Watch what I can do!" they want more than just a moment of attention; they are building their sense of self-worth and identity. One study from Harvard University found that kids whose parents were always there for them had better relationships and were able to handle their feelings better as adults (Shonkoff & Phillips, 2000).

Josh, my youngest son, when he was a toddler is a perfect example of this. To get our attention, he would often stack blocks or do little "tricks." Most of the time, these were trivial things, but Josh's reaction would be much worse when either my wife or I were too busy to give support or notice. He made his actions seem more important when we looked at them or agreed with them, and he would cry or act out when things got too bad. Again, it was a reminder that attention is not just watching; it is a building block for a child's self-esteem and mental stability.

Researchers Gordon Neufeld and Gabor Maté found in 2014 that a child's sense of safety, confidence, and self-esteem is strongly linked to how close they are to their caretakers and how much attention they get. When a kid feels neglected, even in lesser amounts and during normal times, they may become anxious, obnoxious, or emotionally needy. This is the main reason attention is so important for growth.

Why do kids want to be noticed?

(Why we need to connect biologically and psychologically)

I had just started my pediatric training when Lia was born. When I became a dad, I suddenly understood the theories I had been learning about child psychology and human attachment in a whole new way. In the first few years of life, kids depend on their parents or guardians for everything—not just food and safety, but also learning how to behave and have a good relationship with others. Because, biologically, attention means life, they often act in ways that get the attention and closeness of caring adults.

Attachment theory, first used by John Bowlby in 1969 in child psychology, explains this amazing human trait. Babies are designed to connect from the time they are born. Behaviors like crying, talking, smiling, and clinging are all designed to get an adult's attention and care. I saw this early on in all my kids. From the time Lia and Ethan were babies until they were teenagers trying to figure out how to live on their own, they needed attention in diverse ways.

Neurobiological progress has made this need even stronger. Dr. Bruce Perry, a neuroscientist, wrote in 2001 that contact with other people, especially between caregivers and babies, helps their brains and neurons grow. When a baby cries and a parent reacts with warmth or a soothing voice, a positive feedback loop starts. This helps the growth of neural pathways that deal with trust, safety, and controlling emotions.

But the need for attention does not just come from trying to stay alive as a baby. Emotional attachment continues to build a strong psychological base for relationships, self-worth, control, and mental health as a child grows up. When kids ask for attention, whether they do it with words, actions, or emotional shows, they want to feel like they belong and are important in the world.

Think of an example I met Sarah, an eight-year-old girl who was one of my patients. That girl often acted out in class and tried to get her teacher's attention by making a fuss, and it was hard to get her to focus on her homework again. By watching how she interacted with her parents, it was clear that Sarah's dad worked long hours and spent less time at home, and her mom was taking care of two younger babies, even though she meant well. Sarah started to act out more to get attention, good or bad. She felt like she was being overshadowed and ignored. The behavior was not a sign of rebellion; it was a sign of a deeper emotional need that was not being met.

How Parents, Teachers, and Other Caregivers Can Help Kids Who Are Seeking Attention

I have learned that kids will behave differently depending on who we pay attention to, how we react, and how we set limits. This is true whether we are in a busy emergency room or at a noisy dinner table. As parents, guardians, teachers, or doctors, we are not just watching this behavior happen; we are a big part of how it develops and changes.

ATTENTION-SEEKING BEHAVIORS in CHILDREN

I remember a family in the emergency room whose two boys were about the same age as Ethan and Elai. They made me think of how kids often fight for their parents' attention. Kevin, the bigger child, often got into trouble, while Timmy, the younger brother, kept quiet and did nothing. As they talked more, it was clear that Kevin felt pushed to the background by his brother's quiet attitude and the growing attention Timmy was getting for his "good behavior." He learned that getting into trouble was a way to get his folks' attention.

Kevin's case was not the only one like it; I saw similar things happen with my own kids. My fourth child, Maya, often fought for time and attention with her bigger siblings, especially when they were doing well in school or with their friends, which made me, as a dad, pay more attention to those successes. Maya found her own way to get respect at some point, around the time Lia graduated from college. She became extremely competitive at school, not to hurt anyone, but to stand out. As I thought about her behavior, I realized that family relationships can affect how much attention a child wants at different ages.

It will help parents to know that they are not the only ones changing these things. A child's need for and ability to receive attention is also affected by their teachers, the school environment, and the structure of their society. Some of the best ways to stop kids from seeking attention in bad ways are through positive reinforcement, consistent structure, and open conversation about behavior (Kazdin, 2008). Ethan was in the first few years of basic school. He had a teacher who was extremely helpful and gave him specific tasks to do to turn his constant questions and interruptions into leadership skills.

Kids are smart, aware, and overly sensitive to what is going on around them. Children always need to be noticed because it is in their nature to connect with others and stay alive. Parents and other adults who care for kids can give them the attention they want and the approval they need for healthy mental growth by understanding how they are feeling, even when they are having a temper tantrum or a fight with a sibling.

References

Bowlby, J. (1969). *Attachment and Loss: Vol. 1. Attachment.* New York: Basic Books.

Dewar, G. (2013). *Attention seeking or authentic need. Why attention-seeking is normal behavior for kids.* Parenting Science. https://www.parentingscience.com/attention-seeking.html

Kazdin, A. E. (2008). *Parent Management Training: Treatment for Oppositional, Aggressive, and Antisocial Behavior in Children and Adolescents.* Oxford University Press.

Neufeld, G., & Maté, G. (2014). *Hold on to your kids: Why parents need to matter more than peers.* Vintage Canada.

Perry, B. D. (2001). *Neurobiological sequelae of childhood trauma: Post-traumatic stress disorders in children.* In B. van der Kolk, A. McFarlane, & L. Weisaeth (Eds.), Traumatic Stress: The Effects of Overwhelming Experience on Mind, Body, and Society (pp. 253–276). Guilford Press.

Shonkoff, J. P., & Phillips, D. A. (Eds.). (2000). *From neurons to neighborhoods: The science of early childhood development.* National Academy Press.

Chapter 2

Childhood Development and the Roots of Attention-Seeking

There is one thing that all children have in common: they all want to connect with the world around them. When kids want the attention of someone they trust, they do it all the time, whether through laughter, tears, temper tantrums, or quiet pleas for understanding. I have seen my kids—Lia, Ethan, Elai, Maya, and Josh—go through these tough stressful times for sixteen years. These needs were sometimes loud and, in our faces, and other times, they were quiet but powerful signs of a world inside us that we were not always able to see right away.

As a doctor, I have seen the same thing happen in my work. I have seen it in all shapes and sizes, from babies reaching out with tiny hands to older kids trying to impress with bigger moves, whether it is through humor or good grades. Attention-seeking behaviors are not just random acts or acts of trouble; they are often rooted in the most basic parts of a child's development, especially in the early years when important parts of their emotional and mental growth are happening.

This chapter will talk about how early developmental milestones can affect attention-seeking behaviors, how attachment plays a big part in shaping a child's need for attention, and how outside factors like parental responses and early experiences can set the pattern of attention-seeking that a child will have for the rest of their lives.

Figuring out the initial stages of development and how they affect behavior.

Our trip starts in a baby's first few months when most parents are still trying to figure out what every cry, coo, or expression means. A child's first few months shape how they will connect with the world as they grow up.

One of my clearest memories is of when my oldest child, Lia, was a baby. My wife and I were trying to figure out every little thing about her behavior because she was our first child. We jumped if Lia made a noise. Everything stopped when she smiled, and we were happy. She seemed to know that she could count on always getting attention.

We learned that there was more going on than just how we responded, though. Lia was hitting developmental milestones that affected how she behaved, just like all other kids. For instance, babies usually start smiling at other babies around two months old (Beebe & Lachmann, 2014). This is more than just a cute exchange; it is a big step in a child's development as a social worker, showing how attention fuels their emotional drive. Babies know that when they smile, their parents will look at them. It is one of the first ways kids try to get attention and approval, and it shapes how they will interact with the world as they grow up.

Ethan came along a few years after Lia. I was used to figuring out stages of growth by that point, but Ethan's behavior still caught me off guard. According to normal development, Ethan had joined the wonderfully chaotic world of imitation by the time he was one. He copied everything Lia did because, as the younger brother, it got him attention. He did the same things Lia did, like stacking blocks or babbling nonsense words, not only to learn more about his world but also to feel like he was doing something right.

When they are born, children do not depend on words to tell them what they need. Instead, they use their actions, like crying, smiling, waving, and babbling, to show what stage of growth they are in. These signs get more complicated by the time a child is two or three years old. Around age, my third son Elai would throw fits when he did not get what he wanted. This is a normal stage of child development known as the "terrible twos." After a while, I stopped seeing his temper tantrums as disobedience and saw them as a way for him to test limits and see what kind of attention he could get from different actions. His main goal was to make sense of the world that was still changing in front of his eyes.

Researchers who study early childhood development say that actions taken to get attention are not random. They are in line with the cognitive stages that children reach as they grow up (Shonkoff, 2000). From six to eight months, when they learn that objects stay put, to around two years, when they start to show differences in their temperament, children want answers that confirm their presence and place in the world.

Secure vs. insecure attachment and how they change brain structures that seek attention.

As kids age, their attachment styles—whether safe or insecure—shape how they learn to deal with relationships and attention. In 1969, the famous British psychoanalyst John Bowlby said that attachment is an evolutionary need for life. But it is not just about staying alive; it is also about how safe a child feels with the people who care for them.

As a father, I saw this difference even more. Ethan, my second-oldest child, was always happier playing alone than with his siblings. He was more independent from an early age than his brothers. It showed the secure attachment he formed with my wife and me as a baby, knowing he could count on us when he needed us. This gave him the confidence to explore his wants.

Maya, on the other hand, seemed very needy when she was about three years old. She often would not go to sleep unless I was sitting next to her bed. Maya would cry and whine until I came back if I got up, even to get a cup of water. Maya showed some signs of what I might call insecure attachment. This could be because I was busy at work when she was younger.

Attachment events as a baby change the parts of the brain that control emotions and empathy. Research shows that when kids feel safe and comfortable in their relationships, the corpus callosum, a part of the brain that controls emotions, gets stronger. This makes it easier for kids to talk about their feelings (Schore, 2001). On the other hand, if a child does not feel safe with their attachments, their amygdala may activate their fight-or-flight reaction more easily, which can make them more stressed when they are trying to get attention (Schore, 2001).

I have had the chance to work with a lot of kids whose attention-seeking habits were caused by the way they attached to others. Take the case of Danny, an eight-year-old boy who came to me with constant stomach aches that were not coming from his stomach. His father moved a lot for work, so his mother was the main caregiver. He talked about how Danny got worse after coming back from each trip. Danny's actions, like clinging to his dad and becoming more emotional, showed that his uncertain bond with his dad was making him more attention-seeking and looking for comfort.

Children who have a secure attachment are more likely to be able to ask for and receive care in a healthy way. Kids learn how to meet their mental needs and feel more responsible for their lives. Elai's ability to control his emotions improved as he got older. He stopped throwing fits and started focusing on more important things. Instead, children who do not have or do not consistently have a safe attachment, like Danny, will act out emotionally, anxiously, or violently to get attention because they feel like their relationships are not stable. This is especially important for parents to understand: secure attachment does not take away a child's need for care; it just changes how they get it.

How parental responses affect how kids look for attention.

I work as a pediatrician and have had the chance to help many first-time parents figure out why their child is acting the way they are. What the parent does when the child cries out for attention is just as important as the child's own experiences and developmental stages. When a child cries out for attention, that is one thing. When a parent responds, whether they mean to or not, they change the behavior.

How parents react, whether by reacting or rewarding, has a significant impact on how much attention their child gets and how well they can manage it. Ethan, my son, asked a thousand questions every day at dinner when he was in preschool. There was something very curious about him. He asked me and his mother a lot of questions about life, the world, and everything else. When I was tired from a long day at work, I remember saying, "Ethan, not now..." Please wait a moment. Even though his face would fall, he would pick up where he left off minutes later, hoping that this time the question would get my full attention.

My answers made Ethan more aware of the link between persistence and attention, telling him that he had to keep trying to get my attention even after the first failed attempt. In those early years, long before I consciously thought about it, I taught him behaviors that could make him talk too much or feel like he was not being recognized because I was not meeting his needs consistently.

In 1953, the famous behaviorist B.F. Skinner produced the idea of "positive reinforcement," which says that noticing a behavior, good or bad, makes it more likely to happen again. Giving Ethan attention after a lot of questions instead of just a few sent the message that it pays off to keep asking questions. He might have been able to control this need better if I had noticed him sooner.

Similarly, I have seen patients whose attention-seeking behaviors were made worse by inconsistent or exaggerated reactions from their parents. One girl, Grace, who was five years old, picked up the habit of always clinging to her mother when she went out with friends. Grace learned from her family that when she behaved badly, her parents would stop what they were doing to pay attention to her, which made the behavior more likely to happen again. When her younger sibling, on the other hand, did something on their own, she did not get that reaction. Children learn how and when to reach out through involuntary conditioning based on their parents' care or lack of it.

What Early Childhood Events, Relationships, and the Environment Play a Part

As a father of five, I have not only witnessed these important years happen but also lived through them. Even though Lia, Ethan, Elai, Maya, and Josh's genes may have had something to do with their outcomes, the place where they grew up was just as important.

As the oldest child, Lia got the full attention that a baby usually loves when there are no other things going on in the house. When three more children came along, things changed for them. Since Maya and Josh were the youngest, they were always trying to get attention at a house where their bigger siblings were finding stability and ways to enjoy the things in which they were already interested.

Our shared household setting gave each of them early experiences that shaped their personalities in unique ways. I remember Elai pinning a carefully drawn picture to the fridge one day in the hopes of getting compliments. I was so tired after a long shift at the emergency room that I could not even put it into words. I said, "That's nice," half-heartedly while looking somewhere else. Elai, who was only six years old, thought about how I would respond, looked at me longer than I deserved, and then sat down without saying anything else.

The way we treat kids and the setting we create for them, whether we mean to or not, have long-lasting effects on their behavior. When I paid more attention and gave him the specific comments he was looking for, on the other hand, it led to more positive interactions that made him more confident in his creativity instead of hesitant about it.

experts on how to raise kids Rogers et al. (2014) say that a person's mental growth is aided by early experiences that are based on stable, caring, and attentive relationships. How children learn to self-regulate depends on whether they get enough care or not. For example, Josh grew up in a much calmer home than Lia did. This is because I had just finished having four kids and was still remembering how to manage them. When I was raising Josh, I was very aware of how to read his body language and make sure that he grew up in a place that encouraged creative growth without too many reactive traps. This made the entire process more relaxed.

The bonds kids have with their classmates, siblings, and even adults at school significantly impact how far their attention-seeking behaviors go outside of the family. If Elai found that getting compliments on his sense of humor at home helped him do so more at school, that was a sign of the kind of setting we had created.

In conclusion

Children's attention-seeking habits are not just a stage they need to grow out of; they show how their emotional needs are being met and how they are developing physically, mentally, and socially. Understanding these milestones, such as attachment security, parental responses, and the overall relationship environment, can help us better react.

Over the years, I have been a dad and a doctor; I have learned a lot from the good and bad things that kids do to get attention. I have learned that the best way to help kids with these habits is to care for them in a way that supports their healthy growth and gives them the tools they need to get attention in a healthy way, from a place of security and self-confidence.

References:

Bowlby, J. (1969). *Attachment and loss: Attachment* (Vol. 1). Basic Books.

Beebe, B., & Lachmann, F. M. (2014). *The origins of attachment: Infant research and adult treatment.* Routledge.

Rogers, S., Dawson, G., & Vismara, L. (2014). *An early start for your child with autism: Using everyday activities to help kids connect, communicate, and learn.* The Guilford Press.

Schore, A. N. (2001). *Effects of early relational trauma on right brain development, affect regulation, and infant mental health.* Infant Mental Health Journal, 22(1-2), 201-269.

Shonkoff, J. P., & Phillips, D. A. (2000). *From neurons to neighborhoods: The science of early childhood development.* National Academy Press.

Skinner, B. F. (1953). *Science and human behavior.* Macmillan.

Chapter 3

Environmental Factors Contributing to Attention-Seeking

I am the lucky head of a busy family of five, and I have seen my kids deal with the complicated world of family relationships, sibling fights, the allure of social media, and the shaping influence of their schoolmates. Behaviors that are meant to get attention rarely happen by themselves. The setting where kids live can make them stronger, change them, or even quiet them down. This chapter talks about the environmental factors that can lead to attention-seeking behaviors. These factors can come from family relationships, schools, friend groups, and the way we live our lives now that technology is so common.

When I got home from work after a long shift in the emergency room, I would sit down to dinner with all five of my kids and feel like they were all trying to get my attention. Maya would joke that Ethan always got more attention because he was in medical school with me. When Elai was not studying medicine, he was studying biology. He would sneak in his successes to match Ethan's stories about medicine. Josh was the youngest child in the family. He often played fight with his older brothers, to keep from feeling like the baby in the family was forgotten. And because Lia was the oldest and the first to graduate, she often thought it was smart to keep quiet, sure that her accomplishments had already made her famous.

There is a principle that lies beneath these everyday events that we might miss: our children's family and social settings shape not only the outward behaviors they exhibit but also the more inward ones they use to interact with the world. The stage is the world, and kids act out to get attention to interact with and make sense of that social stage.

Family dynamics: rivalry between siblings, fights between parents, and sharing of attention.

Family is often the most important thing that affects a child's growth, and sibling rivalry is one of the most common patterns that lead to attention-seeking behaviors. I can still remember a night at home when Maya was about eight years old, and Elai was just starting to really become a teenager. All day, they fought over small, silly things. Maya would say that Elai spent more time on the tablet than her, but Elai would say that Maya was spoiled because she was the only girl besides Lia.

Their fights made me think of when I was a kid, and my cousin Eric would play with me. As kids, we were raised together, like brothers, and I remember how hard we tried to please our grandparents. I was more interested in sports, while Eric was particularly good at school. He got praise for his grades, and I got praise for how good I was at sports. What we did was not important; what we did to make ourselves stand out—to make sure we got our fair share of approval (Faber & Mazlish, 2004). This competition for attention comes from the way siblings interact with each other. For example, Sharp et al. (2018) found that siblings often compete to keep a shared but separate relationship with their parents.

Getting into fights with your siblings can happen at various times. When it came to Lia, the oldest, there was not much competition, maybe because she was the first. That seemed to make her feel sure about how she was having a good relationship with her brothers. On the other hand, Ethan and Elai were more likely to go up against each other. When Ethan started his journey to medical school, I noticed that Elai would always talk about scientific achievements in college. He would also mention biology in daily conversations, hoping that his story could match or beat Ethan's academic story.

Parents also have an unintended effect on how the family works. I now understand the subtle ways that my wife and I sometimes gave different people less care, even though we tried our best to be "fair." When Lia got that much-coveted first job after college, I often paid her extra attention. Or, when Ethan got into medical school, I would be so proud to talk about his journey in front of guests. Without meaning to, these times can teach the other kids about how attention is shared and what actions will "earn" them more time on the stage with other kids.

Moreover, parenting disagreements can also have a big effect on how kids learn to seek attention. Both in my professional work and in my personal life, I have seen that when parents are fighting, kids often act out to get things back in balance. I remember a boy named Daniel who was nine years old, and I saw him many years ago. They had been getting a divorce for a long time and it was unbelievably bad. Daniel's behavior changed because of the stress. He started doing things on purpose to get in trouble at school, picking fights, and pretending to be sick right before both of his parents were meant to pick him up. Given the situation, it was not a surprise that he tried to get attention by playing out his problems while trying to be heard over the noise his parents were making with their fights (Davies & Cummings, 1994).

In these situations, kids are competing for limited parental attention, which is sometimes split between siblings or stressed by stress from outside sources. This can lead to bad, disruptive behavior that is used to get attention.

What effects do school, peer groups and outside environments have on behavior

According to research, a child's attention-seeking behaviors are shaped by his or her family. At school and with peers, these behaviors are practiced, improved, and changed based on social cues. Kids use the skills they learned at home in real life at school. They do their first big social experiment at school.

This was noticeably clear to me when Ethan and Elai were in grade school. Ethan, who naturally wanted my attention more as a child and was always telling me new things or showing me projects he was working on, was also driven by schoolwork. He did very well in school and often asked his teachers for praise. He did especially well on group projects and was always willing to help.

Elai, on the other hand, liked the company more. He wanted the attention of his friends more than his teachers. I remember getting a call from Elai's third-grade teacher who said that he often got in the way of group work, mostly to make his classmates laugh, rather than to add. Kids who want to fit in but do not know how to do it without drawing attention to themselves often act in ways that are affected by their peers. As I read more about child psychology, I realized that for kids like Elai—who did not get as many compliments in school as his older brother—peer-based approval was just as important as adult approval (Rubin, Bukowski, & Parker, 2006).

When kids start to become teenagers, school and group relationships become especially important. Peer pressure can slowly change habits of attention-seeking into more dangerous areas. When I worked in the emergency room, it was not unusual for teens to come in hurt from risky stunts or attempted stunts. I could always figure out why they did them: they were trying to get attention by doing dangerous but fun things. You want to stand out in front of your peers, even if it means putting your safety at risk. This shows how much your environment affects how you act.

Another girl I worked with was Claire, and she came to the ER after passing out. After a battery of tests showed that she did not have any major health problems, I asked her about her school life. It turned out that she had been under a lot of pressure at school to "play up" her worsening relationship with food, hoping that if her teachers and friends saw how little she was eating, they would feel sorry for her. As a teenager, this became a way for her to be seen, which was a sign of greater emotional and social problems.

From both a personal and a business point of view, I have learned that school is a small version of the bigger world. Children build their identities in this world, which is full of social hierarchies, achievement standards, and group evaluations. The outside world of the school, whether it is good or bad, encourages students to use strategies—like fun, defiance, or striving for perfection—that get people's attention.

Tech and Media: What Smartphones, Video Games, and Social Media Can Do

The time came for my kids to join the internet world. As a parent, I saw how media and technology slowly changed how our family lived. Most of the time, this was true for my younger children, Maya, and Josh. Lia had been a teenager before social media, but Maya and Josh had grown up with technology and were always on their phones or tablets.

Josh, the youngest, would go through times when video games were all he wanted to do. I started to notice how these games changed the way he behaved. This seems like a small thing, but Josh insisted on telling my wife and me what went wrong during a particularly bad game of Fortnite while we were talking about something else. Even though we were not interested, he kept telling us about his gaming problems. It was not so much about the game itself, but about the link and approval he needed as he worked through his anger.

Technology is meant to get people's attention. Smartphones and video games are full-immersion distractions for kids that compete with their parents' attention (Uhls et al., 2014). I saw social media change over time. When Lia was in college, Facebook started to make its way into college groups. By the time Maya was in middle school, Instagram and Snapchat had become the norm for how people talked to each other. In some ways, Maya, and Josh's need for recognition in real life was like what they were looking for on social media: "likes," comments, and interaction. What makes things harder now is that these digital sites have feedback loops that happen all the time, and as parents, we cannot always watch them.

As a therapist, I have worked with a lot of kids and teens whose attention-seeking behavior was based on using social media and video games in dangerous ways. In one case, a 14-year-old boy named Lucas was taken to the emergency room after passing out from being so thirsty. After looking into it, we found that he had been playing video games for almost 48 hours without drinking enough water or eating enough. He had been doing this because he was determined to beat a particularly difficult level. He was not hooked just because he liked games; it was his need to move up the virtual ladders of success that had taken over his life.

In more subtle ways, social media makes this worse. It uses the same emotional parts of the brain as face-to-face communication, giving people dopamine hits in the form of alerts (Montag et al., 2021). Kids get used to looking for approval from people who follow them online and their friends instead of their parents or teachers. The worry is that technology does not just give kids something to look at; it also changes how they see themselves and their place in a bigger, more linked, but still impersonal world.

Things that affect attention-seeking behavior that are cultural and social.

Kids' attention-seeking behaviors are often shaped by the culture and socioeconomic setting in which they are raised, not just what they do at home, at school, or in the media.

As a doctor, I have worked with families from a wide range of cultures and family systems. One thing I have noticed is that diverse cultures have different effects on how kids seek or do not seek attention. I have seen kids from foreign families, for example, act more needy to get approval from their parents and other people, especially when the languages and cultures at school and at home clash.

Sofia, a 10-year-old girl I used to work with for anxiety, came from a bilingual home. Her parents were first-generation immigrants, and they worked long hours to support the family. Sofia often felt pulled between what was going on at home and what was going on at school. She started getting stomachaches before school and had to go to the doctor a lot, but neither her parents nor her teachers could figure out what was wrong. I finally understood that Sofia's "illness" was a quiet cry for attention because she felt disconnected from her parents because they had become used to the cultural norms of home, and she often felt "foreign" at her very American school (Chao, 1994).

The kids' social class can also have a big effect on how they act in these situations. Kids from lower-income families may seek attention for varied reasons than kids from wealthier families. Often, it is because they do not have as much parental contact or access to resources. Children in low-income families may fight for attention when their parents are too busy with work and other tasks, even if they try their best (Bradley & Corwyn, 2002). When this need is not met, it leads to behaviors like crime or dropping out of school that are meant to get adults to interact, even if it is in a bad way.

On the other hand, kids from better-off families may try to get attention by overachieving or being too perfect, where doing well in school becomes the currency for praise. I sometimes see this trend in my own kids as well. Ethan and Elai, for example, sometimes competed for academic honors. Even though they had all the tools and help they needed, the low-income environment in which they grew up still shaped their need for attention. It is not just about money that counts here; it is also about how time and emotional resources are shared within the home.

In conclusion

Children are not silent observers of their surroundings; they interact with and react to the many things going on around them. The things they do to get attention show that they need to connect with others, be noticed, and feel supported. These things are all facilitated by their environments. The setting our kids are in has a significant impact on how they look for approval and attention. This includes family rivalries, school competition, the impact of screens, and larger societal norms.

As parents, caregivers, and professionals, knowing about these influences helps us respond more consciously and make decisions that either support or lessen unhealthy attention-seeking behaviors. Most importantly, it helps us give kids the space and approval they need, without any competition, conflict, or digital distractions.

References

Bradley, R. H., & Corwyn, R. F. (2002). *Socioeconomic status and child development.* Annual review of psychology, 53(1), 371-399.

Chao, R. K. (1994). *Beyond parental control and authoritarian parenting style: Understanding Chinese parenting through the cultural notion of training.* Child development, 65(4), 1111-1119.

Davies, P. T., & Cummings, E. M. (1994). *Marital conflict and child adjustment: An emotional security hypothesis.* Psychological Bulletin, 116(3), 387-411.

Faber, A., & Mazlish, E. (2004). *Siblings without rivalry: How to help your children live together so you can live too.* HarperCollins.

Montag, C., Lachmann, B., Herrlich, M., & Zweig, K. (2021). *Addictive features of social media/messenger platforms and freemium games against the background of psychological and economic theories.* International Journal of Environmental Research and Public Health, 16(14), 2612.

Rubin, K. H., Bukowski, W. M., & Parker, J. G. (2006). *Peer interactions, relationships, and groups.* In N. Eisenberg (Ed.), Handbook of Child Psychology (pp. 571–645). John Wiley & Sons, Inc.

Sharp, C., McCabe, K., & Herbert, L. (2018). *Family functioning and children's behavioral symptoms in child day treatment.* Family Process, 57(3), 705-720.

Uhls, Y. T., Michikyan, M., Morris, J., Garcia, D., Small, G. W., Zgourou, E., & Greenfield, P. M. (2014). *Five days at outdoor education camp without screens improves preteen skills with nonverbal emotion cues.* Computers in Human Behavior, 39, 387-392.

Chapter 4

The Different Types of Attention-Seeking Behaviors in Early Childhood

----

Being a parent to five kids over the course of twenty years has taught me something important about how they act: attention is something they need from the start. The need for attention is always there, even if they look for it in diverse ways, sometimes directly and sometimes indirectly. As a doctor with more than 18 years of experience, a lot of which was spent in the busy emergency room, I have seen a lot of diverse ways that kids want attention from their parents and other people in their lives. Some of these are clear and loud, while others are quieter and less obvious. But they are all important.

I remember very clearly how hard my son Ethan worked when he was a baby to keep our attention on him. Ethan was an outgoing kid, and he would never think twice about cutting me off in the middle of a talk or pulling my shirt off to ask me one of his famous "why" questions. I found it annoying at times, especially after a long shift

ATTENTION-SEEKING BEHAVIORS in CHILDREN

in the ER, but I quickly realized it was not because I did not like being interrupted. Ethan was just trying to keep my attention and keep him linked in a meaningful way.

Then my fourth child, Maya, came along. Her ways of getting attention were quite different. Maya planned things better. There is no question that she could have a temper tantrum, but most of the time, she used emotions to get what she wanted. I laugh now when I remember how she would cry big, fake tears whenever something went wrong, like when she did not get the ice cream she wanted. It was not just emotional immaturity; she was carefully practicing the art of showing how upset she was to get the attention she wanted.

I have learned that a child's desire for attention can show up in diverse ways, each with its own difficulties and meanings, through both professional observation and personal experience. This chapter will talk about four diverse types of attention-seeking behaviors that happen in early childhood: acting out in class or talking too much, crying, temper tantrums, and clinginess; passive attention-seeking by withdrawing and refusing to engage; and emotional manipulation by guilt-tripping and exaggeration.

Young children who cry, throw tantrums, and cling around.

There are not many scary things that happen as a parent more than the first time your child has a temper tantrum in public. You know what I mean—usually it is a crowded place like the grocery store, post office, or something else where people who are not parents forget what it is like to deal with a screaming child.

Elai, my third child, used to throw tantrums all the time when he was younger. Around age two, kids start to have the "terrible twos," and I remember this one event very clearly. He saw the rack of brightly colored candy near the register after we were done shopping for groceries. It made me cry so hard that I had to lie on the floor of the grocery store and scream, "But I need it!" repeatedly. Pediatricians and most parents know that kids that age are just starting to learn how to be independent. So far, they have not learned how to control their feelings. Elai's temper tantrums were just his way of showing how angry he was that he was not getting the attention and results he wanted.

Tantrums are often very tiring for parents, but they are not always stubborn behavior. Portugal and Davidson's study from 2003 says that temper tantrums are a child's body, showing how hard it is for them to handle too much emotion. It is how they talk about unmet needs or wants that they do not have the words or emotions to say quietly yet.

But kids do not always throw fits when they want attention. One less obvious but still difficult trait I noticed in Maya as soon as she learned to walk was her tendency to cling to things. When Maya was with other people or in a new place, she did not want to be alone for long. Even at family reunions, where she was with her family and friends, she would circle the room with her arms outstretched and beg, "Daddy, carry me," repeatedly if she could not find me or her mother after a few minutes. This kind of clinginess shows how much a child needs to feel safe. It became clear to me that Maya needed more care when I was home during times when I had to spend more time at the hospital for work. She used her behavior as an emotional guide to connect with her caretaker, which made her feel safer and more stable.

Behaviors like crying, temper tantrums, and clinginess are not just random; they are ways for kids to deal with stress and stay close to you. Usually, they come from fear, anxiety, anger, or feeling unsafe, and they let parents know what their child really needs emotionally. Understanding the "why" behind these actions can be frustrating, but it helps parents and other adults who care for kids to respond instead of just reacting.

Acting out: talking too much, disrupting class, and being too active

One day, Josh's teacher called me. He was about six or seven years old. She began, "He's smart, but, doctor, Josh talks ALL the time." He wants the attention of the whole class. This behavior happened at home too, like when Josh would interrupt family meals to tell a dramatic story about something that happened at school, even when the talk was not about him. This did not surprise me. That behavior did not work so well at school, though. Josh's talking too much, cutting people off, and even his silly jokes were not just ways for him to express himself; they were attempts to get attention and stay in the center. Children who act in these ways, like Josh, are often trying to be at the center of what is going on because they are afraid that if they do not, they will be forgotten or ignored.

As a child psychiatrist, I have worked with a lot of kids whose parents were worried about how bad their behavior was at school. Teachers would say that students often lost their temper, fidgeted too much, or talked too much during lessons. People who need attention often act out in ways like being hyperactive or making a lot of noise in class. As parents, it is easy to think of it as just unruly behavior, but a child's overactive energy is often caused by problems with peers or adults in charge.

A boy named Kevin, who is seven years old, was a good example of this. Kevin often caused problems in class because he moved around a lot and could not concentrate on one thing for more than a few minutes at a time. His mother brought him to the clinic at first because she thought he might have ADHD, but after talking with both Kevin and his teacher for a long time, I decided that his behavior was more about making sure people knew he was there than about uncontrolled hyperactivity. Kevin had two older siblings who were both very smart. His outbursts were ways for him to find his own identity and get respect that he did not always feel he got at home.

Cheung (2017) examined children's classroom behavior and found that talking too much, being too active, and being interrupted are often signs that children are either not getting enough to do or are looking for approval from their teachers or peers. For kids like Josh or Kevin, their actions reflect a deeper need to feel important and safe in their social surroundings.

Passive Attention-Seeking: Withdrawal, Refusing to Do Things, and Being Shy

Some kids do not need to yell to get your attention. In fact, silent withdrawal is one of the sneakiest ways to get attention. Even though my daughter Lia is usually sure of herself, she became shy when she was in middle school, right after we moved to a new city. Josh's attempts to get attention were louder, but Lia was quieter and harder to pick up. She stopped actively participating in school clubs, which was something she used to enjoy. Instead, I often found her just sitting in her room, unwilling to join family dinners or hang out with her brothers. This seemed strange to my wife and me, but Lia's teachers did not say anything about behavior problems. Over time, it became clear that her absence was just a passive way for her to get attention. She was not acting out; she was just pulling away, hoping someone would see her and pull her back in.

In my practice, I have seen this passive type of attention-seeking a lot of times. Emily is a shy seven-year-old whose parents were worried because she would not play with other kids in her class. Emily's case stands out. Emily did not bother anyone, cry, or have temper tantrums, but her teacher noticed that she always sat alone during group tasks and avoided eye contact a lot. Being shy and not wanting to be around other people were ways for Emily to figure out where she fit in her family and the world. This became clearer after she talked to her parents more. There was a new younger child in the family, and her passive behavior was partly a reaction to the change in attention in her home.

When children do quiet things to get attention, they often hope that the adults around them will notice and connect with them emotionally. This is easy to miss because, unlike temper tantrums or other problems, it does not always need instant attention. But the mental need to connect is still extraordinarily strong, and this is where caregivers should pay extra attention.

Being shy or distant can be a sign of anxiety or insecurity, which can be caused by things like moving, the birth of a child, or changes in the way the family works. Coplan and Arbeau's research from 2008 shows that kids who are shy or quiet often show small signs that they want attention. Even though they are shy around other people, these kids still need to know that they are important and valuable in their social world, but they do it in quieter, less obvious ways.

Emotional Manipulation: Making people feel guilty, exaggerating, and using emotions to get their attention.

Maya started crying one day when she was about five years old. My wife and I refused to buy Maya a new toy, and right away she did her well-rehearsed act of shaking lips, wide, teary eyes, and whispering, "You're so mean to me." She was fine before I told her I was not mean and that we could not afford the toy right then. She was also fine after I told her that. The best way to get someone to do something is to play on their emotions.

Emotional influence is a skill that can be learned, especially in younger children. The first step is to realize that strong feelings, especially angry ones, can get a parent's attention faster than simple requests. Maya figured this out very quickly. She knew that making her sadness or loss worse made her feel more accepted. They use similar strategies when they talk to their caretakers, which is true for many of my young patients. Matt, a five-year-old boy I worked with, had produced a more extreme version of this plan while going to the doctor. Matt's mother said that he often made her feel bad by telling her, "You didn't let me play my game today—don't you love me anymore?" He would lose all his regular energy, and his face would change to look incredibly sad suddenly. The behavior was broken down and it was clear that Matt was mentally negotiating for more screen time by making his mom think about the effects of her choices.

To get attention, people use emotional trickery, such as making adults feel guilty, exaggerating, or putting on an incredibly happy or incredibly sad show, to change how they react. The child is just learning which emotional switches make an adult cry (Juang et al., 1997), so it is not malicious. Children, especially those who are still growing, use their feelings to negotiate with others. This kind of behavior usually goes away once they learn better ways to talk to others, but it can happen in early childhood.

Kids who have learned that being emotionally intense gets parents to respond faster are more likely to feel guilty. People need to see this for what it is: a way to get the attention of a tired parent who wants to get rid of the problem as soon as possible. To break the circle of emotional manipulation, you need to be aware of the behaviors and set clear, calm limits without giving in to the emotional drama.

In conclusion

Behaviors that are meant to get attention are a normal part of growing up and can happen at any age or stage. All these behaviors—loud crying and temper tantrums from babies, trouble at school, and quiet withdrawal from others by shy kids—come from the same place: a need to be seen, heard, and accepted. I have seen these habits show up in diverse ways in my kids and patients because I am both a dad and a pediatrician. Figuring out why a child is acting out can help you decide whether to see their behavior as a problem or as a way for them to get your attention and feel connected.

By learning about these diverse types of attention-seeking behaviors, parents can better react with understanding and patience, while still helping their kids find better ways to talk about their feelings and needs.

References

Cheung, K. (2017). *Classroom Management: Perspectives of Disruptive Students' Behaviors in Primary School Education.* Journal of Educational Psychology, 78(2), 320-334.

Coplan, R. J., & Arbeau, K. A. (2008). *The Stresses of Shyness in Early Childhood.* Journal of Abnormal Child Psychology, 36(3), 359–371.

Juang, L. P., Zimmer-Gembeck, M. J., & Alger, S. A. (1997). *Emotional manipulation in childhood sibling relationships.* Child Development, 68(3), 207-213.

Potegal, M., & Davidson, R. J. (2003). *Temper Tantrums in Young Children: Behavioral Composition and Temporal Organization.* Journal of Developmental and Behavioral Pediatrics, 24(3), 140-147.

Jordan R. Chavez IV, M.D.

Chapter 5

The Emotional Drivers Behind Attention-Seeking

As the years have gone by, I have learned how complicated kids' attention-seeking habits can be. Some parents, like me after long shifts in the emergency room, are tired and might think these behaviors are just acts of resistance or mischief. People often think that the behaviors will go away if they just give that one extra lesson or are a little stricter. But now that I have five kids—Lia, Ethan, Elai, Maya, and Josh—and have worked as a doctor for hundreds of kids, I start to think more deeply about why a child acts out to get attention. What is really going on at the heart of those actions? What unfulfilled mental needs are they trying to meet?

Understanding the mental causes of attention-seeking behavior is not plainly important; it is essential. Kids do not act out, run away, or overstate their feelings for no reason. Often, they are talking about things they might not be able to say aloud, like worry, fear, loneliness, and nervousness. How someone acts, not always what they say, tells the best story.

Maya, my smart but sometimes over-the-top emotional daughter, is a good example. If Maya thought that someone else was getting too much attention as a child, she would naturally try to get it back. I remember a family event where she felt shy around her older brothers because they were so successful. While Lia was excited about graduating with honors from college and Ethan was talking about how hard medical school was, Maya, who was about fourteen at the time, suddenly became very "upset" that no one had praised her dress. She almost cried because she wanted to change the subject. On the surface, it looked like pride or acting without thinking. Maya, on the other hand, was talking about a deeper need: the pain of feeling unnoticeable.

In this chapter, I will talk about the feelings that lead to these kinds of actions. Attention-seeking is often more of a cry for help than a sign of rebellion. This is because people who do it are often afraid of being left alone, feel insecure, have unmet emotional needs, or have neurodevelopmental problems like ADHD or autism.

Neglect, fear of being left alone, and loneliness.

One of the most basic needs in people, especially children, is to feel seen, cared for, and linked. This is where the emotional need for attention often comes from. When those needs are not met, kids will do anything to be close to their parents or other adults who care for them. A few years ago, I took care of a young boy named Sam who had been to the emergency room several times for what his parents called "mysterious" stomachaches. There was no physical cause when they took him to their family doctor. Now, they wanted to see if something more important was being missed.

I talked to Sam's mother for a while to learn more about what was going on with his claimed illness. As it turned out, Sam's dad had recently started working longer hours, so Sam had been seeing him alone more. It so happened that his stomachaches happened when his father was most busy or not there. It became clear that Sam was not sick; he just felt emotionally empty. His worries about being left alone and not being valued or recognized were showing up in his body.

Fear of being left alone and feelings of being ignored often show up in kids as various kinds of attention-seeking behavior. When Maya acted out her feelings, she was showing a less obvious form of this. We tried our best to give each child equal attention, but she sometimes felt like she was not getting enough because she had four brothers. When I felt the need to be validated, sometimes by making a small crisis, it was because I was thinking, "Am I important?"

Even if it is just a small thing that makes a child feel ignored, they will look for other ways to get the caregiver's attention. Bowlby (1969) says that crying fits, temper tantrums, and being needy can be a child's unspoken way of dealing with feelings of being alone and disconnected. If you do not do anything about it, these habits could get worse and turn into behavior problems as they get older. When there are substantial changes in the family, like a new sibling coming home, moving, or a parent's work hours changing, feelings of loss can lead to dramatic attention-seeking behaviors.

While Sam and Maya showed mild emotional demands, some kids act in a way that is more obvious and bothersome. In the emergency room, I saw a case of Jessica, a five-year-old girl who had been brought in after a fit of crying and hyperventilating because her parents were fighting. Jessica's parents were having problems in their marriage and did not know how much their arguments were affecting their daughter. She slowly saw their arguments as a sign that she was being left behind. Seeing her parents unhappy or withdrawn made her worry that they would leave her too. What looked like a need for attention was really a fear of being alone, which showed up as chaos.

We should always remember that carelessness is not always done on purpose. Children and caregivers need to feel emotionally connected to each other, and even small, unintentional cracks can leave a big hole. To fill that hole, children may act out or be manipulative.

Attention-seeking behaviors are caused by anxiety, insecurity, and a lack of confidence.

Anxiety is another strong feeling that leads to behaviors that are meant to get attention. Most of the time, when a child does not know where they stand in their family, school, or social group, they act out in ways that get attention to find out. Anxiety can show up in many ways, such as talking too much, having unhealthy habits, or doing the same things repeatedly to calm down. For people who feel insecure, trying to calm down can mean being too active, withdrawing, or putting in too much effort.

I noticed that Elai was becoming more competitive with his older brother Ethan around the time he was becoming a teenager. It was not in the healthy way that makes siblings competition fun, but in a quieter, more tense way. Teachers at school noticed that Elai was giving answers more often, even when he was not sure of them, and then he would give long explanations for why he might not have been "completely wrong." At home, when people were talking about Ethan's progress in medical school, Elai would interject stories about his own biology major problems, looking for approval.

Elai was not trying to brag; he was dealing with his feelings of fear. He felt pressure to match or beat the achievements of his brothers because he came from a family with many high achievers. Deep-seated worries about where he stood in the hierarchy came to the surface as competitive drive. Elai's behavior that got him attention was caused by his worry about being "just as good" as his smart brothers. He needed someone to see how valuable he was, not just as another part of the family's academic relay race, but as a unique person with his own skills.

People who came to see me also showed this trend of wanting attention that is linked to anxiety. One case that stands out is that of Taylor, who was nine years old and always "forgot" her chores, even though she got good grades overall. Her folks were incredibly angry with her and thought she might just be lazy, but the truth was more complicated than that. Taylor had patterns of constant worry, especially before tests or when the teacher was judging her. For some reason, her "forgetfulness" was both a way to get closer to her parents and a way to keep herself safe. By not doing her homework, she could escape the stress of doing badly on it.

As Dr. Thomas Ollendick's (1998) writings show, kids often act out in ways that get their attention and make them feel safer with their caregivers when they are feeling insecure or afraid of failing. When these kids cling, ask a lot of questions, or do the same thing over and over, they are showing their parents that they need approval more when they are feeling the most uncertain.

The Link Between Not Meeting Emotional Needs and Outward Behavior

Over the years that I have worked in pediatrics, this link has become clearer to me: when kids' emotional needs are not met, they do not just go away. Instead, they find new life in how people act around them. This is not just about obvious unruly behavior; it can include a wide range of actions, from rebellion to withdrawal, from intense competition to complete lack of interest.

As an example, I remember taking care of twin boys named Daniel and Sean. They were always together but had quite different personalities. Daniel, the "squeakier wheel," always had a lot of energy when he went on trips. He asked a lot of questions and wanted to be approved of by both his parents and his friends. On the other hand, his brother Sean was quieter and liked to stay out of the way. I was interested in their differences because I saw them often at the clinic for monthly checkups.

Sometimes, their parents told me about a problem Sean had been having at school. He was not acting badly; he just disappeared into the background. He was not taking part in class events and rarely raised his hand. When asked how he was doing with making friends, he did not give many answers. His mother said, "He's just so quiet. I don't know how to get him to talk."

The truth was that Sean's behavior to get attention was not flashy because he had taken the opposite approach—he stayed out of sight and avoided being seen. He let his unmet emotional needs for connection and confidence show through withdrawal instead of temper tantrums. He learned how to be shy to get people's attention from his twin brother Daniel. When looked at more closely, both boys were showing the same unmet need—validation—but they were reacting in opposite ways.

A famous psychologist named Dr. Ross Greene wrote in 2008 that kids' actions, like resistance, clinginess, or even withdrawal, are often signs of how they feel inside. When kids do not have the mental tools to fully understand or talk about their unmet needs, they use their behavior to show what they want. Whether at school, at home, or with friends, the child may act like they are up to no good, but deep down they may be feeling empty or unsafe and cannot put it into words.

What problems with mental health, like ADHD, autism, or trauma, have to do with wanting attention

Some actions that people do to get attention are not just caused by feelings of anxiety or lack of confidence. Sometimes, these behaviors are made worse by mental or neurodevelopmental disorders like autism, ADHD, or disorders linked to trauma. As a doctor, I have seen a lot of kids who were seeking attention not because they were upset, but because of how their brains were processing what was going on around them.

Take ADHD as an example. There was a lot of energy in both Ethan and Elai, but they had different personalities. As a doctor, I know how to tell the difference between kids who are just continually active and those who have ADHD because of their hyperactivity, restlessness, and impulsivity. Everyone who knew Matthew, the young child I took care of, said he was smart and kind. His teachers said, though, that he was always talking over other people, interrupting, and getting up in class for no reason. If you do not know much about ADHD behaviors, this might seem like an intentional attempt to get attention, which in a way it was. This behavior was not an act of defiance, though. It was Matthew's way of dealing with his impulsive brain, which acts before it thinks about the effects.

Executive failure makes it hard for kids with ADHD to control their behavior, which often causes them to act out in ways they cannot fully control to get attention. They feel the need to act and talk so quickly that their actions become attempts to get attention right away, even if that is not what they mean (Barkley, 2014). Matthew was not really interested in praise, but the behaviors he had trouble controlling showed that his brain wanted it.

In the same way, kids on the autism spectrum may do intense, repetitive behaviors to get attention, and they often put a lot of value on order and routine. There was a kid named Jake who needed attention so badly that he would ask me repeatedly about his everyday life. Not once, but ten times, he asked his mom, "Is it time for school now?" even though she had already told him when they were leaving. Jake's autism made him think about the world in a way that was not like most people who are insecure act to get attention. He had trouble dealing with changes in his surroundings, which led to his need for reassurance and attention.

Stress and trauma can also make these habits worse, but in quite diverse ways. To protect themselves, some kids who have had traumatic or unfavorable childhood experiences (ACEs) act out by wanting attention all the time. I took care of a girl named Amara whose father died when she was incredibly young. Her mother told how Amara would wake up the whole family in the middle of the night by crying for no reason or asking to be with someone even when it was safe. Amara's actions were not just because she wanted to be with someone; they showed a deeper, almost unconscious fear of being alone and losing someone, which came from her trauma.

Studies have shown that stress can mess up the emotional centers of the brain, making kids act out or withdraw to get attention to deal with their unstable emotions (Perry & Szalavitz, 2006). These kids are dealing with the long-term emotional effects of their stress without even realizing it. They do this by avoiding people or being very alert all the time. Attention-seeking cycles help them feel emotionally stable again.

In conclusion

Whether it is Maya's flair for drama or Sam's physical signs of attention-seeking, kids' attempts to get attention are not just about disobeying or needing attention. Most of the time, these habits are caused by worries, fears, unmet needs, or even deeply rooted neurodevelopmental patterns. When we understand the emotional and psychological complexities behind attention-seeking, it not only makes us better parents but also helps us react more understandingly in our jobs as professionals or caregivers.

Kids talk about their actions long before they are self-aware enough to use words to describe how they feel. As parents, caregivers, or in my case, as both a father and a pediatrician, the challenge is not to stop these behaviors. Instead, it is to see past them and meet kids where they are, making sure they feel seen, safe, and mentally always fed.

References

Barkley, R. A. (2014). *Attention-Deficit Hyperactivity Disorder: A Handbook for Diagnosis and Treatment*. Guilford Press.

Bowlby, J. (1969). *Attachment and loss: Attachment*. Basic Books.

Greene, R. W. (2008). *The Explosive Child: A New Approach for Understanding and Parenting Easily Frustrated, Chronically Inflexible Children.* HarperCollins.

Ollendick, T. H. (1998). *Childhood Disorders: Behavioral-Developmental Approaches.* Taylor & Francis.

Perry, B. D., & Szalavitz, M. (2006). *The Boy Who Was Raised as a Dog: And Other Stories from a Child Psychiatrist's Notebook--What Traumatized Children Can Teach Us About Loss, Love, and Healing. Basic Books.*

Chapter 6

The Role of Parenting Styles in Attention-Seeking

As a father of five and a doctor, I have learned that there is no "one-size-fits-all" way to be a parent. What works for one kid might not work at all for another. Lia, my oldest, was naturally responsible and independent. Ethan, my second child, on the other hand, was more needy and often needed a lot more reinforcement. Elai, my third child, seemed to do best with calm consistency, while Maya, my fourth child, looked for ways to connect emotionally that were more subtle and artistic. Josh, my youngest child, was usually quiet, but he had a distinct way of getting people's attention when he needed to. It takes a lot of skill to be a good parent, and sometimes it is hard to find that nice balance.

As a doctor, I have learned that the way parents raise their kids has a big effect on how they try to get attention. How a caretaker responds to a child's pleas for attention affects not only their behavior at the time, but also their mental and social growth in the future. This includes whether they give in too easily, are strict, or do not pay attention at all.

I will talk about how authoritative, permissive, authoritarian, and careless parenting styles affect kids' attention-seeking behavior in this chapter. We will also talk about the risks of extremes, like giving too much or too little attention, and how parents who do not set clear standards can cause kids to use even more complicated ways to get attention. Finally, and most importantly, I will share what I have learned over the years about how to set limits and communicate in a way that supports a child's need to connect, not undermine it.

Diverse types of parenting: authoritative, permissive, authoritarian, and neglectful

As pediatricians, we often use well-known ideas of child development when we tell parents what will work best. Diana Baumrind's parenting styles model from 1966 is a well-known and recognized framework. It describes four main types of parenting: authoritative, permissive, authoritarian, and neglectful. Each of these types influences how kids act, especially when they want to be the center of attention.

1. Is authoritative parenting the best way to raise a child?
I can think of one case that I think shows what happens when parents are strict. Maya, who was eight years old, came to the clinic a lot during the years I treated her. Her family stood out to me because of how calm, well-behaved, and sure of herself she was. Maya had to miss all her school soccer games this season because she broke her arm in an unbelievably bad accident. I remember that she dealt with this tough situation with strength, which I think shows how strict her parents were.

Mom and Dad were strict but nice to Maya. They did not just break the rules for no reason, but they did explain things. The doctor told Maya she could not play soccer for a while, and she understood why.

Her parents understood her anger but did not give in to her cries or demands. When she told her parents that she was upset or annoyed about missing out, they were understanding but strict. They told her to think about what she could do and told her she would be back on the field soon. Maya did not pull away or complain more; instead, she changed. Her need for emotional support was met, but she was not given too much.

Parents who are authoritative set fair limits and encourage emotional warmth and open conversation. Studies have shown that kids whose parents are strict tend to behave less needlessly when they want attention. This is because their emotional needs are met regularly, making them less likely to use disturbing behaviors to get attention (Baumrind, 1996). These kids know that their caretakers are there for them without being too strict or too lax because they have clear rules and are loving.

2. Being a permissive parent, or the "yes" parent

Even though strict parents set reasonable boundaries, I have also seen the other side. Ethan, my nephew, is the best example of what can happen when a parent gives in too much. Ethan loves his parents very much. On the other hand, I could tell that they had a lax parenting style from the outside. It was normal for Ethan to do whatever he wanted, like stay up late, eat whatever he wanted, skip chores, and leave toys all over the house. There was not much order, and the limits were almost nonexistent.

At one family get-together, he was the center of attention for all the wrong reasons. He had temper tantrums after temper tantrums because he did not want to share his toys with his cousins. Instead of setting limits, his father constantly gave in, promising Ethan new toys and unrestricted screen time to calm him down. He gave him whatever he wanted to avoid the headache. It briefly calmed things down, but it also made Ethan more likely to use temper tantrums as a strategy. Ethan learned that throwing a fit was the fastest way to get his parents' attention and favors, so he did these things repeatedly.

Baumrind's (1966) theory of permissive parenting describes the "soft" method, in which limits are not clearly defined and authority is not very present. Because they know they can get anything by pushing boundaries, these kids are more likely to act out to get attention, and sometimes their behavior can get so bad that it is called manipulation. A kid who is constantly told "yes" struggles to control their emotions, which makes them feel unstable and like they need more attention. They also do not have the tools to understand why limits are important.

3. Parenting with a lot of authority: The Drill Sergeant

Authoritarian parenting, which some people might call "strict" or "militant," is on the other end of the range. I saw this personally with Diego, a nine-year-old boy who came to see me with headaches and stomachaches that would not go away. As I investigated Diego's physical problems, it became clear that a lot of his worries came from home. Diego's father was extremely strict, with extremely high academic standards and little tolerance for failure or even average performance.

Diego's dad used "tough love" with him. He expected everyone to do their best in school. If you got a C or even a B, you got in a lot of trouble and had to do extra work on the weekends. People saw Diego as well-behaved outside of the house, but when he got there, he would lose control and cry for hours or beg his father to forgive him for small mistakes. It turned out that Diego's stomachaches were caused by anxiety. His body was reacting to the stress of always having to meet his strict father's standards and seeking comfort from his mother to get attention away from the strictness his father demanded.

Children who grow up in strict families may behave perfectly in public, but when they are not around strict parents, they often act in ways that are meant to get attention, just like Diego. Kids who grow up in these kinds of homes learn that breaking down is the only way to release mental stress, which makes them act worse when no one is around. When parents are authoritarian, they value obedience over warmth and do not allow for much emotional flexibility. This can have major psychological effects as kids seek attention in unhealthy ways (Baumrind, 1996).

4. Parenting Without Caring: The Void
But sometimes the worst behaviors do not come from being too strict or too lax—they come from not having any standards or care at all. As a pediatrician, I have had the terrible chance to work with kids whose parents were neglectful, which means they were not there for them emotionally and were emotionally distant. A 12-year-old boy named Jaden made a lasting impact. He had been to the emergency room several times with injuries he had caused himself, ranging from cuts and broken bones. When he came back for a third time, I became worried and worked hard to figure out what was going on.

Jaden's story broke my heart. His parents were emotionally but not physically missing a lot of the time. His life seemed uninteresting all the time because both were busy with work and personal problems. Jaden's behavior problems, like getting into trouble at school or hanging out with the wrong people, were not really an act of rebellion. Instead, they were a way for him to get attention from people who did not give it to him.

A common result of parents who do not pay attention is that their kids learn that any attention is better than none (Maccoby & Martin, 1983). This is what happened with Jaden. Theresa Wiseman's (2017) research on the subject shows how long-term neglect can make a child act badly toward themselves and be emotionally unstable as they try to deal with not having any care.

What are the problems with extreme parenting?

Overindulgence vs. Under-Engagement
As a pediatrician with years of experience, I have also seen parents who are very indulgent and not involved enough. An interesting fact is that both extremes can make kids act more attention-seeking, though in diverse ways.

Too much pampering

When a parent is overindulgent, they give in to their child's every wish, even if it means teaching them how to control their impulses and wait to get what they want. It has been my experience to see kids who grow up in homes with lots of toys, gadgets, and activities that never end. But there is often a different story going on inside these houses. A six-year-old girl named Lily was one of these kids. She came into my office often asking for new toys and getting incredibly angry when her wishes were not met right away. Lily's mom told her that she had never heard the word "no" when it came to her wants and needs.

Overindulging can teach kids that they need to feel good right away for every mood, but it does not help them learn healthy ways to deal with their feelings. Instead of learning how to deal with loss or absence, kids who are given too much may use attention-seeking behaviors like temper tantrums or guilt-tripping to get what they want (Clarke, Dawson, & Bredehoft, 2016). For Lily, her parents, even though they meant well, kept telling her that she could quickly get rid of any problems by getting more stuff, which slowed down her mental growth.

Not Engaged Enough
On the other hand, parents who are emotionally or physically unavailable may not seem like a clear problem but can be just as harmful. Jacob, a ten-year-old boy I worked with, came from a family that was not incredibly involved. His parents, who were both working adults, took care of his basic needs but were not interested in his daily life, school, or friends. While he was shy in class, Jacob was an incredibly quiet kid who acted out to get attention at home, especially with his parents. He would cling to them and beg for approval in ways that seemed almost desperate.

As I have learned in my professional and personal life, children need more than just care (Shin et al., 2016). They need to be emotionally, socially, and intellectually engaged. When they do not get this, they are more likely to back down or step it up, often turning to defiance or extreme behavior to get the attention of their missing parent. Kids try to fill the void left by not being engaged in activities in almost any way they can.

How expectations and rules that are not always followed can make people seek attention

Inconsistency is one of the most important things that has changed the behavior of both my own children and pediatric patients. The structure is good for kids, even if they do not like it. When rules, standards, or discipline change without warning, it can cause emotional confusion, which can lead to more attention-seeking.

Maya was the most aware of when things were not going as planned among my children. It was hard for our family to stick to our habits during a time when my work hours in the emergency room were very unpredictable. Maya acted up sometimes and got away with it, mostly because I was too tired to say what would happen. Some days, I lost it much more quickly and turned small problems into bigger punishments because I was too busy. During this time, I saw that Maya's need for attention got worse. She showed defiance in subtle ways that made me deal with her actions, which drew me into her inner world, but it was not real rebellion. Instead, she was responding to how her emotions were not always stable.

In contrast, I remember working with a seven-year-old boy named Ethan whose parents had a tough time enforcing rules consistently. On some days, they had to carefully follow their family rule and not use screens for more than an hour. On days when both parents were tired from work, Ethan could watch TV for hours without anyone coming in to check on him. This lack of stability made Ethan's attention-seeking behaviors more unstable, especially when limits were randomly put back in place, which made him push back in ways that were not acceptable.

Eisenberg et al. (2001) and other studies have shown that kids who do not receive regular discipline are more likely to act out and cause problems when they try to get their caregivers to respond more predictably.

Creating healthy boundaries and ways to talk to your kids

So, the question is, how can we, as parents, help our kids keep their emotions in check? How can we create a place that discourages the worst kinds of stubborn attention-seeking? Over the years, I have learned a lot about how important it is to set healthy limits and communicate clearly by raising five strong-willed kids and getting to know many patients and their families.

My spouse and I did our best to talk to our kids clearly and regularly. There was open discussion about not only what was expected but also why it was important. This helped everyone, whether it was Lia figuring out how independent she was after college, Ethan and Elai dealing with their family rivalry during pre-med classes, or Maya learning how to control her emotions.

This way of thinking also applies to my young patients. There was a boy named Lucas who would often use emotional manipulation to get the attention of his parents. Because she was often too busy with work and housework, Lucas's mother found it easier to react to his over-the-top sadness or anger than to talk to him when he was thinking more clearly. Over time, I helped her set clearer goals and have more structured talks. I also told her how important it was to figure out how he felt before he tried to manipulate her.

Parents who encourage open communication and set clear, unwavering limits can stop a lot of attention-seeking behavior. Kids need to know that there are safe structures in place, but that does not mean they should be controlled harshly. It means sticking to the rules while allowing emotional expression in safe, healthy places (Gottman, 2011).

Kids do well when adults who care for them set fair limits, connect with them on an emotional level, and have deep conversations with them about what is important. Parents need to carefully plan their kids' mental environments and help them grow by being patient, understanding, and always the same.

In conclusion

Being a parent is undoubtedly one of the hardest things to do, but how we deal with it has a direct effect on how our kids act, especially when they want attention. Whether they are permissive, strict, overindulgent, or not involved enough, the way parents raise their kids affects both their behavior and their emotions.

As a dad and a pediatrician, I know that there are no right or wrong replies and that mistakes will be made. But the most important thing is to keep a balance that helps our kids' hearts and minds: between structure and flexibility, between discipline and empathy, between communication and limits.

References

Baumrind, D. (1966). *Effects of authoritative parental control on child behavior.* Child Development, 37(4), 887–907.

Baumrind, D. (1996). *The discipline controversy was revisited.* Family Relations, 45(4), 405–414.

Clarke, J. I., Dawson, C., & Bredehoft, D. J. (2016). *How Much Is Too Much? Raising Likeable, Responsible, Respectful Children—from Toddlers to Teens—in an Age of Overindulgence.* Da Capo Press.

Eisenberg, N., Chang, L., Ma, Y., & Huang, X. (2001). *Relations of parenting style and its consistency to children's externalizing and internalizing behaviors.* Psychological Inquiry, 12(2), 217-228.

Gottman, J. M. (2011). *Raising an emotionally intelligent child: The heart of parenting.* Simon and Schuster.

Maccoby, E. E., & Martin, J. A. (1983). *Socialization in the context of the family: Parent-child interaction*. In E. M. Hetherington (Ed.), Handbook of child psychology: Socialization, personality, and social development (pp. 1-101). John Wiley & Sons.

Shin, S. H., Miller, D. P., & Teicher, M. H. (2016). *Exposure to Childhood Neglect and Physical Abuse and Developmental Trajectories of Heavy Episodic Drinking from Adolescence to Young Adulthood*. Drug and Alcohol Dependence, 165, 237-244.

Wiseman, T. (2017). *The long-term effects of childhood neglect*. Journal of Child Psychology and Psychiatry, 54(4), 489–500.

Chapter 7

Attention-Seeking Behaviors in Adolescence

Teenage years are a time of substantial changes for both teens and their parents. I have seen a lot of teens struggling with who they are in the pediatric emergency room. Often, they do things to get attention that make their parents confused. I have dealt with this reality directly at home, where I have watched my five kids navigate the rough waters of adolescence with varying levels of maturity and, sometimes, mischief.

As they got bigger, Lia, Ethan, Elai, Maya, and Josh all had their own set of emotional needs, wants, and needs for attention. But as their father and a doctor, what really struck me was how their ways of getting attention changed a lot when they were teenagers. Kids used to just say things like, "Look, Dad! I got an A on my math test!"

to get their parents' approval. Now, they say more complicated things to get approval from their friends. Friendships became especially important, social standing became especially important, and the usual desire for parental care took a back seat to the need to be accepted by their peers.

The teenage years are confusing but valuable for a person's growth. This is when kids figure out who they are. Most of the time, wanting recognition is a big part of that process.

In this chapter, we will discuss attention-seeking behaviors in teens. We will discuss how teens shift their focus from parental approval to peer validation, the risks and rebellion that come with their need for attention, how social media makes that need stronger, and how attention-seeking behavior is a big part of how teens form their identities.

The Change from Seeking Attention from Parents to Seeking Attention from Peers

Everyone who is a parent has had that moment when they realize they are not the center of their child's world anymore. Little by little, questions like "Dad, what do you think?" are swapped out for "Ethan says that" or "Chelsea thinks that." It is both a sad and important change for parents like me.

This change first became clear to me when Ethan turned thirteen. Ethan had always been eager to make me happy, whether it was by doing well in sports or showing off his test scores. But now he was looking for approval from his friends instead. Although I used to be his main audience, it became clearer that his friends were now the ones who were meant to see his shows.

Ethan was about fifteen years old when he came back from a school basketball game with a bigger-than-usual sense of self-importance. There was nothing we said to make him so happy. He was just smiling. During the game, his classmates cheered him on and called him "the MVP," which made him more popular with his peers. I then understood what was going on: Ethan's actions meant to get attention were now aimed at his peers. For him, acceptance from them was more important than mine.

Developmental psychology provides extensive information on the transition from wanting attention from parents to wanting attention from peers. Erik Erikson's stages of psychosocial development from 1950 show that the identity vs. role confusion phase occurs frequently during youth. At this especially important age, teens constantly seek approval from outside sources, increasingly from their friends rather than from their families. Teenagers change how they think about themselves by seeing how their friends see them (Erikson, 1968).

For parents, this change can be hard because it can feel like they are losing control, but for Ethan, and most teens, it was a natural step toward freedom. As pediatricians, we tell parents that this time of growing apart is an important part of their child's development toward becoming independent adults. As teens get older, getting approval from their parents is less important to them than building their social standing, which they can do through humor, success, or even rebellion.

Elai had a similar experience. Elai has never been the loudest or most attention-seeking kid in our family, but when he was in high school, he suddenly cared a lot more about what his peers thought. This change was especially hard for me at family meals, where Elai, who is usually quiet, did not try to get approval from us but put on a great social show when he talked to his friends. During that time, he became friendlier, more active, and more focused on rising in the eyes of his peers.

I learned that the key was to stop being the one who gave outward validation and start being the emotional safety net. Teenagers may not act out to get attention at home as much as they used to, but that does not mean they do not look to their parents for security when their relationships with their peers fall apart.

Teens' Behaviors That Are Risky, Rebellious, and Driven by Results

When teens want to get attention, they often do risky things. I learned a lot about this while working in the emergency room. It seemed like every year, teens were hurting because they did dangerous things, like jumping off a roof for a "challenge" on social media or trying drugs to impress their friends.

This made me think of a 16-year-old boy named Kevin who was taken to the emergency room after trying an extremely dangerous skating trick. He broke his wrist and, when questioned, said that the challenge—a dare from his friends and an attempt to be filmed for social media—had pushed him to do it. Kevin was performing for an audience that could not be seen. He wanted to get praise from his friends and even some strangers who would see the movie online.

Research by psychologists like Laurence Steinberg (2010) shows that teens take risks to show who they are and to get noticed by their peers. But it is important to remember that they are not always breaking adult rules. Often, they are trying to show themselves and their friends that they are brave, bold, or able to push the limits. Many kids who take risks and act based on performance do so because they want to oversee their friends.

This was also clear to me from my time with Maya. Maya was the most emotional of my five kids, especially when she was a teenager. I remember how, as soon as she got her driver's license, every chance to "run an errand" became a chance to show how independent she was. Maya's friends would pile into the car and drive off. Sometimes they would speed down country roads with the windows down and music blasting as they enjoyed their newfound freedom. Maya was not driving so recklessly that she ended up in the emergency room, but she did some dangerous things to show that she was the brave, independent teen. This was especially true when her actions were close to being rebellious.

Not all teens will break the law or do dangerous things just for fun. But for those who do, it is important to know why they act that way. Taking risks is not always a conscious act of rebellion. Often, people do it to get attention or make their independence known.

During the teen years, people also become more focused on performance, whether it is in school, sports, or social situations. This was clear in Elai, a naturally competitive kid who felt the need for more praise for his academic success. He worked hard not only to get his parents' approval but also to keep up with his friends. He used school to test his skills. Elai's academic success was as much about showing his worth to himself as it was about making a name for himself in his social group.

Teenagers do not always put themselves in real danger when they take risks. For some, it could mean risking their grades. Teenagers may sometimes put too much pressure on themselves by trying to meet impossible standards set by others or by themselves to feel accepted. As pediatricians or parents, we need to understand that these habits, whether they are dangerous or too much work for school, are all part of the same bigger plan: the desire to be noticed.

Social media and teens' need for approval from others
Teenagers today may be more obvious in their need for attention on social media than anywhere else. In the last ten years, social media has changed the way teens grow and change in a whole new way. When she was younger, my oldest daughter, Lia, did not use social media much because people in her group still valued face-to-face interactions more. But for Maya and Josh, Instagram, Snapchat, and TikTok were a big part of their teen years.

I remember Maya carefully managing her social media accounts for hours on end, her phone always by her side. There were obvious signs of her need for attention on social media that made them stand out to me. She "performed" every post she made, whether it was a picture in a trendy outfit, a funny video meant to get "likes," or a story meant to show off her social life. Like most parents my age, I was skeptical of social media at first, but I quickly learned how important it is for shaping how teens and young adults interact with each other. Maya saw social media as more than just a stage. It was like a never-ending auditorium where her friends and even strangers watched her try to find her place in the world and figure out who she was.

I found it interesting that Josh used social media in a quite unique way. Josh was more passive than Maya, who eagerly sought approval from others through likes and comments. He read, responded, and scrolled, but he never posted. But it became clear when I asked him why he was so focused on his phone: it was not to add to the conversation, it was just to watch it. Josh was looking for some kind of approval by staying linked, making sure he was never left out of any social activities going on online, even if he was not the one posting.

For teens today, apps like Instagram and TikTok are extensions of who they are. They help them build their personalities and get feedback from others right away (Uhls et al., 2014). For many people, each "like" is a sign that they are seen, valued, and linked. It is hard to tell the difference between performance art and social exchanges on these platforms. This makes teens want more attention, often by showing filtered versions of their lives. In a way, social media has made the natural desire for approval from peers stronger by making attention-seeking habits more common around the world.

However, this need for approval comes with its own problems. Too much attention-seeking on social media can make people feel very inadequate when they are not recognized or when comparisons become too strong. This has happened to several of my patients. A girl named Lily came to see me because she had started to feel anxious after being bullied online. Her self-esteem depended on how people responded to her online, which made her always look for more extreme or exaggerated ways to show who she was. It is not a surprise that social media makes underlying fears much worse, even in teens who are well-adjusted.

As doctors and parents, we cannot ignore how social media affects the way teens act when they want attention. We need to teach people how to use technology safely and support activities that boost self-worth in ways that go beyond short-term online approval.

As a person grows, they form their identity and look for attention.

Finally, we need to understand that teens' attention-seeking habits are not always bad. In fact, these actions are deeply connected to one of the most important parts of being a teenager: figuring out who you are. Teenage years are a time when children change into young men and women. During this time, boys and girls often do things that get attention, whether they are loud or quiet.

Ethan was the best example of this for me when he was a late teenager. Like many kids his age, Ethan was having trouble figuring out who he was and what he wanted to become. He started to play around with different ideals, hobbies, and things to talk about. For one week, he was deeply interested in sports, the next in music, and suddenly, he was interested in medicine. He did this to see which version of himself would stick.

In many ways, wanting attention helped him "try on" these distinct roles. Whether it was by doing well in sports or getting praise from his teachers, Ethan was carefully building a sense of who he was that needed feedback from the outside world. Teenagers' actions that are meant to get attention from others give them important feedback that shapes their identity. These actions show them which traits are accepted and encouraged and help them avoid traits that are not.

Erikson (1968) and other psychologists have long studied the role of puberty in shaping identities. Teens use their desire for attention, whether from their friends or on social media, to figure out their jobs, their values, and who they are as individuals. It is important to understand that attention-seeking behaviors can be a normal part of growing up, even if they show up in ways that bother or upset parents.

In conclusion

The teenage years are a wonderful, difficult, and often scary time for both kids and their parents. Teenagers may act out more to get attention, especially from their friends or because they want to do well in school, but these actions are a normal part of growing up and becoming more independent. Teenagers can try out various parts of their identities during this time, from taking risks to getting approval on social media. This can be frustrating for the adults in their lives at times.

It is our job as parents and pediatricians to kindly guide them through this process. We should know that wanting approval from others is a normal part of being a teenager, but we should also encourage healthy ways of expressing ourselves, feeling good about ourselves, and having healthy relationships. If we know about these drivers, we can talk to our teens without criticizing them and instead with kindness and understanding, giving them the help they need to get through life safely and well.

References

Erikson, E. H. (1950). *Childhood and Society*. Norton.

Erikson, E. H. (1968). *Identity: Youth and Crisis*. Norton.

Steinberg, L. (2010). *Adolescence.* McGraw-Hill.

Uhls, Y. T., Michikyan, M., Morris, J., Garcia, D., Small, G. W., Zgourou, E., & Greenfield, P. M. (2014). *Five days at an outdoor education camp without screens improves preteen skills with nonverbal emotion cues*. Computers in Human Behavior, 39, 387–392.

Chapter 8
Identifying the Root Cause of an Individual Child's Attention-Seeking

----

I still remember the first time it dawned on me: Kids do not always act in ways that get attention in the same way. I learned this lesson the hard way when I had five kids: Lia, Ethan, Elai, Maya, and Josh. All my kids had their own unique ways of getting my attention. Over time, I learned that behaviors that seemed like simple attempts to get attention often had deeper emotional causes. During the loud cries for attention, acceptance, or validation, there were often deeper reasons why children kept drawing attention to themselves.

On the other hand, Lia was usually responsible and did not try to get attention like her brothers did. I will always remember how tense she seemed the night before her first big job interview after college. "What if they don't like me? "She said it in a whisper as she joined me for a late-night snack in the kitchen. Even though she was sure of herself, she was just trying to get attention because she needed to feel safe. At that point, I realized that attention-seeking was not always about rebellion or drama; it could be subtle and just mean someone needs mental support.

On the other hand, Maya, who was smart and quick-witted, often used dramatic style to get people's attention. During one family reunion, Maya yelled that no one had praised her dress because everyone was talking about Ethan's time in medical school. It was not the dress itself that made her so upset; it was feeling like she was ignored. It took me a while to understand that her actions were not based on vanity or selfishness but on a greater need to be noticed.

As much as I loved being a pediatrician, I also loved being a parent. I learned to recognize attention-seeking habits and more importantly, to figure out what they were really trying to tell me. Key things that helped me both at home and in the emergency, room were paying close attention to trends and what set them off and getting help from professionals when I needed it.

This chapter will show you how to figure out why someone is acting out to get attention, whether they are complaining, being dramatic, or being defiant. It breaks down the discovery process that every worried parent, teacher, and pediatrician needs to go through. It starts with noticing patterns and understanding what sets off these behaviors. Then, it moves on to figuring out when these behaviors become problematic and when to work with behavioral and mental health professionals.

Keeping an eye on attention-seeking behavior patterns and triggers

It is easy to spot attention-seeking behavior in kids, especially if you know what to look for. I have learned this from being a parent to five kids and working as a doctor. Once you know what sets a child off, it is easy to see that there is more to a child's movements than meets the eye.

As Ethan got older, I noticed that his need for attention was not always there. It would come up at certain times, especially when he was not sure about something. Ethan, for example, lost some of his usual confidence as he studied for his first set of medical school tests. He would start talking about medical terms during dinner as a test to see if he could surprise the rest of the family. This is what I started to call a "mini performance." At first, I thought, "Well, he's just bragging." But as I heard more, it became clear that Ethan was not being cocky; he was just trying to reassure himself that he knew enough to do well on his upcoming tests.

When someone is trying to get our attention, the first thing we should do is look for patterns. When does this start to happen? What is going on right before or after the child acts out or cries out for attention?

When I am with a patient, I often try to figure out what is going on behind the behavior by looking beyond what they are doing. One case that stands out is a girl named Lily. She started having regular emotional outbursts in class when she was about seven years old. Her teachers said she was annoying and could not concentrate, and she often demanded attention in ways that kept her classmates from paying attention. I asked her parents to write down the times when she had these fits. What we learned was remarkably interesting: Lily mostly acted out when her plans changed, like when there was an unexpected fire drill or a replacement teacher in the morning. Lily's temper tantrums were not just an attempt to get attention; they were a response to the stress she felt when her daily pattern changed. Just like Ethan, her need for recognition was caused by feeling insecure.

Parents and caregivers can better understand why certain behaviors occur by tracking behavior trends and finding triggers. It is not always about the attention but rather the instability, anger, or feeling of being too much to handle on an emotional level. As both a therapist and a parent, I tell caregivers to dig deeper. Often, the time sends a message.

However, patterns are not always so obvious. For example, Maya felt pushed to the background by her smart brothers. I kept asking myself, "What happens before Maya starts wanting attention?" Over time, the pattern became clear: it always happened after a family event where her brothers' achievements were compared to her own, who was going to college and working hard. Maya was not just a drama queen; she was also trying to fix what she saw as an unfair distribution of attention.

The first step to finding the underlying cause of attention-seeking behavior is to recognize these trends and triggers. This does not just mean watching the behavior; it also means figuring out what makes it happen.

How to Tell the Difference Between Normal and Abnormal Attention-Seeking

Of course, different people will seek attention in diverse ways. Some kids, like Maya, use it to fix what they see as unfair support. In the case of Ethan and others, it may come from a need for comfort during times of doubt. But every parent knows that there is a difference between wanting attention in a healthy way and doing things that start to hurt relationships or school life.

I often think about Devon, a boy who was one of my first young patients. Devon's actions to get attention were not like the usual problems that happen in most classes. He often threw temper tantrums at home and at school, not just when he was mad, but also when he thought no one was paying attention to him. His parents were worried, which was understandable since his behavior was hurting his schoolwork and relationships with other people. Teachers said Devon's outbursts often stopped whole class talks. He also had trouble making close friends because other kids avoided him because of his unpredictable behavior.

In Devon's case, his increasing need for attention was not only regular childish behavior; it had become a problem. At that point, it was time to figure out if the behaviors were a sign of greater emotional problems or even developmental problems.

There are three main things that can help you tell the difference between normal and unhealthy attention-seeking: frequency, intensity, and effect. Does the action only happen sometimes, or does it happen all the time? How bad is the child's need for attention? Does it cause temper tantrums and a lot of emotional drama? Does the behavior get in the way of their daily life, like at school, at home, or with other kids?

Josh, my younger son, mostly liked getting attention. One classic example was his occasional outburst of anger when one of the bigger kids made his accomplishments seem less important. Josh would talk over his family when they were talking about Ethan's trip to medical school or Elai's academic success. He would also interrupt or overreact to trivial things, like how well he did on simple class projects. Still, his behavior never got so bad that it caused a big problem. It was just part of the normal difficulties of siblings. He only wanted his share of attention.

When attention-seeking has big effects, like hurting relationships or grades, it changes from being normal to being a problem. Kids like Devon often show early signs of long-lasting attention-seeking behaviors that need help from adults, teachers, or experts.

Structured observations can help parents determine when attention-seeking becomes a problem. If behaviors get in the way of daily life, especially social or classroom activities, it might be time to start using more structured answers or get more help.

Performing tests and talking to behavioral or developmental experts

ATTENTION-SEEKING BEHAVIORS in CHILDREN

Once parents notice a trend of bad attention-seeking behavior, they must ask themselves, "What do we do next?"

As a father and a doctor, I have always emphasized initiative and investigation. A child's need for attention can be a sign of a deeper problem, like anxiety, a mood disease, or trouble paying attention. Detailing evaluations and talking to the right experts can help find the deeper reasons behind a child's behavior.

In psychiatric work, I have seen this very clearly. For example, Devon was finally sent to a child psychologist who helped figure out that he had ADHD. He acted impulsively and could not control his emotions well, which led to his outbursts and attention-seeking behaviors, especially in places where he had to concentrate for long amounts of time. If his parents knew more about how his actions are related to his neurodevelopment, they could help him learn better ways to control them.

When a child's attention-seeking behavior gets out of hand, as a pediatrician, I work with behavioral or developmental experts. If parents, teachers, or other caregivers notice upsetting trends in a child's attention-seeking behavior, a full assessment is the next step. For example, teachers and parents may fill out checklists and watch how the child acts, and child psychologists or behavioral specialists may do official evaluations.

For example, Lily, the girl who had meltdowns when her routines were broken, had higher levels of worry when things did not go as planned, according to an evaluation done by her parents, her teacher, and a child psychologist. Once her parents realized that her need for attention was caused by stress, they learned how to slowly introduce structured plans and help Lily get used to changes in her routine, which made unexpected events less stressful for her.

Sometimes, kids may even need to see speech therapists, physical therapists, or developmental pediatricians to find out what is wrong, especially if their need for attention is related to problems with processing sensory information or communication delays. Every one of these tests helps to give a full picture of why a child acts the way they do.

It is not enough to just examine the action; you need to also examine why it happens. Parents and professionals can find meaningful answers for kids' problems when they act like detectives and piece together the puzzle of their emotional and behavioral world.

Working together with mental health professionals to take a more complete approach

As pediatricians, parents, and teachers, we sometimes see attention-seeking behaviors that cannot be fixed with simple notes or one-time talks. These actions can sometimes be signs of deeper emotional or mental needs. When this happens, working together with mental health workers is necessary.

Professionals like psychiatrists, psychologists, and qualified counselors have special tools that can help parents and kids learn more about the mental causes of unruly behavior. When I work with families, working with mental health workers has made all the difference in the world.

I remember a young case named Emma whose need for help had gotten so bad that it was scary. At school, she always pretended to be sick to avoid talking to her friends, and she would often exaggerate light pain to get to the school nurse. Her teachers told her parents they were worried about how she was acting and how often she needed to be alone to get attention. We learned that Emma had unrecognized social anxiety, and her behavior that was meant to get attention was mostly a way for her to avoid getting into a fight with her peers.

Together with a child counselor, we were able to help Emma learn better ways to control herself and deal with her social issues. Emma's parents learned how to act in a way that supported her healthy ways of coping while also finding the underlying cause of her anxiety through therapy. The need for attention was not the problem; it was a sign of a bigger problem that needed to be dealt with by a psychologist.

In a different case, a boy named Tim acted very rebelliously and craved attention, to the point of being rude. Collaborating with his parents and a mental health team, we were able to figure out that some of his behavior was caused by depression that had not been identified. Tim was treated with both therapy and medication with the help of a child psychiatrist. This helped him deal with some of the mental problems that led to a lot of his unruly behavior.

Mental health workers can help with attention-seeking behaviors in ways that are hard to achieve with medication, discipline, or behavior charts alone. They teach us, both parents and doctors, to look past the behavior and deal with the child's feelings.

In conclusion

Figuring out why a child is acting out to get attention is not always easy, but it is especially important. Children and the reasons they want attention are not the same, just like children. As parents, pediatricians, and caregivers, we can respond with intentional and effective behavior management while meeting the child's deeper emotional needs. We can do this by carefully observing patterns, telling the difference between normal and problematic behaviors, and getting help from specialists when we need it.

Seeking attention is not always sad; it is just a way for kids to show they need social connection, reassurance, or approval. As parents and experts, it is our job to understand these behaviors with compassion and find out what is really going on underneath. Working together with mental and behavioral health professionals when needed lets us give the best, most complete help possible.

References

Baumrind, D. (1996). *Effects of authoritative parental control on child behavior.* Child Development, 37(4), 887–907.

Erikson, E. H. (1968). *Identity: Youth and Crisis.* Norton.

Gottman, J. M. (2011). *Raising an emotionally intelligent child: The heart of parenting.* Simon and Schuster.

Steinberg, L. (2010). *Adolescence.* McGraw-Hill.

Uhls, Y. T., Michikyan, M., Morris, J., Garcia, D., Small, G. W., Zgourou, E., & Greenfield, P. M. (2014). *Five days at an outdoor education camp without screens improves preteen skills with nonverbal emotion cues.* Computers in Human Behavior, 39, 387–392.

Chapter 9

How to React to Attention-Seeking Behavior (Short-Term Strategies)

Attention-seeking habits are normal parts of parenting or working with kids. Every parent and pediatrician will ask themselves, "How should I respond in the moment to attention-seeking behaviors?" This is true whether the behavior is a subtle comment meant to make someone feel bad or a full-on temper tantrum in the middle of the grocery store. It is important to find a balance between giving the child the care they need and stopping them from doing things that are annoying, manipulative, or bad for them.

I have raised five kids and worked as a doctor for almost twenty years, so I have seen attention-seeking behavior from both sides. At home, with my kids Lia, Ethan, Elai, Maya, and Josh, and at work, in the emergency room, with people of all ages. There is no one way to deal with attention-seeking that works for all kids or all situations. It is important to react carefully and regularly.

This chapter will give you some short-term, useful ideas for dealing with attention-seeking behavior in a way that makes the child feel valued and supported while also dealing with the unruly behavior without adding to it. Parents and healthcare workers need to be aware of and balanced when dealing with these behaviors. This includes using positive reinforcement, keeping calm, and setting clear limits.

How positive attention works to stop unruly behavior through reinforcement.

This is the one piece of advice that has helped me, and many other parents deal with attention-seeking behaviors: give positive attention early and often. Positive feedback is a wonderful way to get your child to behave better and help you talk to them more clearly.

During Elai's early teenage years, I did not like how he had to talk about family events without reason. While Lia liked to talk about her college activities and Ethan liked to talk about his medical school accomplishments, Elai always felt like he had to beat everyone else. He would speak up, trying to get the conversation back on track by telling stories about his biology classes that were more interesting than they really were. At first, it was annoying to me. I would scold him sometimes, which, as you might guess, made things worse. But one day, my wife told me I should try something different.

I made it a point to pay attention to Elai at the start of the talks instead of waiting for him to speak up. Before anyone else could speak, I would ask Elai, "How was your lab this week?" as dinner was being served. I heard you were working on a cool project.

This initiative-taking changing of attention worked well. When Elai was fully and honestly acknowledged, he cut people off a lot less often. I was not trying to reward him for interrupting, but I was trying to give him valuable feedback at a time that worked for the whole family. The reason Elai was acting out to get attention was not to cause trouble; it was because he wanted to be noticed. The main need he had was met when I paid attention to him before he acted out instead of during them.

This rule can explain many different kinds of behavior that are done to get attention. When a child behaves well, positive feedback can come in many forms, such as thoughtful verbal praise, physical touch (like a reassuring hand on the shoulder), or even just making eye contact. It makes them more likely to do good things to get respect instead of sad things (Kadin & Rotella, 2021).

Parents or other adults who care for kids should not wait for unruly behavior to happen before responding to it. Instead, they should try to predict when their child needs attention and deal with it right away. By rewarding good behavior before it turns bad, you not only show the child you value them, but you also help them find healthier ways to get support.

How calm leadership and patience can help calm things down.

Taking charge of behavior that is trying to get attention from a calm leading position has a huge effect, especially when emotions are high. Children can notice a lot of emotions and will often act like the people around them. That is, if you lose your cool, they will make things worse.

As a father and a pediatrician, I have had this tried many times. An event that stands out is when my daughter Maya, who was about seven years old at the time, had a major meltdown at a family picnic. At the beach, she made a big sandcastle, but the waves broke it. Maya is usually extraordinarily strong, but she broke down in tears and anger and demanded that everyone "fix" the problem or make her a new one.

At first, I wanted to jump in and fix the problem myself, which is something many parents do in a hurry. But I stopped and realized that Maya's outburst, while caused by real disappointment, was really a cry for attention. I led with patience instead of adding to the problem by being angry. I did not scold her right away or even fix the castle right away. Maya was upset, so I carefully told her that the sandcastle would not last forever and that building it was part of the fun. As soon as I sat down next to her in the sand, I began building a new castle. She joined me slowly but surely.

Setting a good example of how to deal with her feelings calmed Maya down.

This idea works just as well in clinical situations. A parent can easily go into panic mode in a busy emergency room full of angry or scared kids. Lucas, five years old, had been to the doctor more than once with small injuries, such as bumps, scrapes, a small fall from a dining room chair, and other similar things. Lucas was trying to get attention by crying a lot while talking about his injuries and demanding that everyone in the room look at him.

Lucas's parents loved him, but they seemed to go back and forth between being overprotective and irritated. During one visit, his mother looked incredibly stressed, and Lucas could tell, which made him act worse. I quietly took charge of the situation. I told Lucas I knew he was hurt, but in a way that made him feel better. Instead of giving him the strong emotions he was showing, I cooled them down with calm commands in my voice and body language. While Lucas may have still been hurting, he did not feel the need to act out more to get attention right away.

By staying calm and collected, we show kids—whether they are our own or our patients'—that it is possible to deal with anger and rage without losing control.

How to Set Limits That Work Without "Feeding Into" the Behavior

The structure is good for kids, even if they do not always like it. But that structure does not come from making rules or setting emotional limits out of anger or frustration. Instead, there should be clear, purposeful limits that a child learns to work around.

One of the more minor but important things parents and caregivers need to know is how to set limits without adding fuel to the attention-seeking fire. Even if we want to be strict, when we show our frustration, scold, or give long-winded comments, we unintentionally reinforce the behavior we are trying to stop.

I remember a time when Ethan and I were together like this. As a medical student, it is hard for me to remember my quiet son as a naughty 12-year-old who liked to play tricks and push the limits all the time. One time that stands out, Ethan wanted to be noticed, so he made faces at the dinner table while the rest of us were trying to talk. He was not publicly defiant, but he knew just enough to make us act.

It was tempting to use a long reprimand as a teaching moment, but I knew that making the talk last longer would only give Ethan what he wanted, which was attention. I chose a different path instead. Ethan, stop," I told him in a strong voice. I told him, "You'll miss out on dessert if you keep going," when he would not stop. After that, I left it at that. There was no argument or wrangling; there was only a calm limit with a clear outcome.

He finally gave up after a few more seconds of being stubborn. He eventually learned that there was no reward for continuing when boundaries were made clear and not argued. This was true no matter what the joke or test of patience was. When there was unruly behavior, the faster I could apply the consequence and the less I interacted with the behavior, the faster it stopped.

It is easy for parents to give their kids too much attention by rubbing their hands or telling them why their behavior is wrong. Feeding into the cycle can be avoided by keeping answers short, clear, and calm. The goal is to keep them interested enough to show that there are limits, but not so much that they get any more attention that would make them want to behave badly.

In my professional work, this has helped a lot when I am working with kids who are used to having temper tantrums or complaining repeatedly. Setting clear rules for certain behaviors, like what kinds of accidents need to be taken to the emergency room or how to manage non-urgent issues with confidence, helps kids and their parents understand that certain actions will not lead to extreme responses. The limits are set and are always being reaffirmed.

Responses Right Away to Two Types of Attention-Seeking: Disengagement and Detachment

One of the trickiest parts of parenting and caring for someone is figuring out when to interact with attention-seeking behavior and when to step back. If you do not think things through, the wrong response—either too much involvement or total disengagement—can easily backfire.

When it came to my daughter Maya, I learned the hard way that some habits needed attention, and others did better with a quiet distance. Maya was a lot more dramatic than her brothers, and she often tried to get people to feel what she felt. She would say over-the-top things like, "No one saw how hard I worked on this drawing," when she was younger to get people to respond. At first, I would jump in with eager promises. But as time went on, I realized that keeping these small problems going only made things more intense. At these times, it was important for me to keep some distance—I could understand how she felt without getting too caught up in them.

I stopped dropping everything to focus on her drawing and telling her how great she was for doing so. Instead, I said things like, "I'm sure everyone appreciates your hard work, Maya." After that, I did not let the discussion go any further. This short acknowledgement followed by a subtle distance let her know that I appreciated her efforts while still being firm in my belief that the world did not spin around one person's need for constant approval.

Genuine involvement, on the other hand, is often the smartest thing to do. One of these kids in my practice was named David. He was terribly busy and often yelled for attention, but not in a funny way. He did it because he was bored and lonely. After spending time with him, I learned that his frequent meltdowns at school were caused by him having trouble in school and always feeling like he was falling behind. His desire for recognition was not an act; it was a cry for help that was not being met elsewhere.

In situations like David's, it was important to be involved, not detached. Someone who would listen to him and point him in the direction of tools he could use to control himself was what he needed. I showed his parents and teachers how to deal with his outbursts by actively fixing problems instead of passively ignoring them. Knowing that some actions are signs of deeper needs that might not be met if we pull back completely was key in this case.

Getting the right mix between not caring and caring is both an art and a science. Parents need to know how to tell the difference between when their child needs emotional help (through real involvement) and when the behavior is just getting better because it is getting so much attention.

In conclusion

When you are dealing with attention-seeking kids, you must walk a fine line between correcting the behavior and not encouraging the very things you want to stop. Positive reinforcement, calm leadership, and clear, constant limits are all early ways to help kids change both short-term behavior patterns that are just for attention and longer-term, more persistent ones.

How you respond to kids trying to get your attention can have a significant impact on how they deal with their need for attention, reassurance, and recognition in the future, whether you are a parent, pediatrician, or teacher. We give our kids the tools they need to manage their growing emotional worlds more freely and in a healthy way by knowing when to give them positive attention, when to interact with them in a warm way, and when to calmly set firm limits.

References

Kazdin, A. E., & Rotella, C. (2021). *The Kazdin Method for Parenting the Defiant Child: With No Pills, No Therapy, No Contest of Wills.* Mariner Books.

Gottman, J. M. (2011). *Raising An Emotionally Intelligent Child: The Heart of Parenting.* Simon & Schuster.

Baumeister, R. (2018). *The Power of Bad: How the Negativity Effect Rules Us and How We Can Rule It.* Penguin Random House.

Chapter 10
Preventing Attention-Seeking Behaviors (Long-Term Strategies)

As a pediatrician who has worked in emergency rooms for a lot of years, I have seen a lot of different attention-seeking habits in kids and teens. There are greater emotional reasons behind many of these actions. It could be a need for approval, a way to deal with stress, or just a desire to connect with others. And finally, as the dad of five kids—Lia, Ethan, Elai, Maya, and Josh—I can say from personal experience that attention-seeking is not just "acting out"; it is often a child's way of letting you know they feel seen or heard.

It became clear to me, both in the office and at home, that long-term plans are needed to stop problematic attention-seeking. Some of these tactics are building emotional intelligence, encouraging healthy ways to show emotions, and being clear about what is expected of everyone. As we talked about in the last chapter, short-term strategies like detachment or calm leadership can help stop immediate behaviors. But if we want to stop attention-seeking in the long term, we need to make sure that our kids feel safe, emotionally connected, and able to talk about their needs in healthy ways.

Long-term ways to stop attention-seeking behavior include making strong emotional connections, teaching emotional intelligence, showing others how to have healthy relationships, and being clear about rules and standards. These personal stories from my work, my family, and the lives of coworkers and friends will help us build a sturdy base so that we do not have to pay too much attention to it in the first place.

Creating strong emotional bonds to cut down on the need for too much attention

Building a strong emotional link with kids from an early age may be one of the best ways to stop them from constantly wanting attention. When kids are sure that the people in their lives will meet their emotional needs without them having to act out to get attention, they are less likely to do sad things just to get attention.

When I think about emotional bond, Jenny, a child patient of mine, comes to mind. Jenny was six years old when I met her. She had been to my emergency room several times for stomachaches and other problems that did not seem to have a clear medical cause. A number of tests ruled out any big physical problems, which made me think that her problem might be emotional instead of physical. Jenny was not spending enough time with her parents one-on-one, which was clear from talking to them. Jenny felt mentally pushed to the side because she had to care for a new sibling and her parents both worked full-time. Her stomachaches were her way of calling for attention.

I told her parents that they should spend more personal time with Jenny. That is not just time, but time that is emotionally present. I told them not to look at their phones while sitting next to Jenny at the dinner table. Instead, I told them to pay full attention to Jenny while they played games, asked her about her day, and gave her their full attention, even in small ways. Jenny stopped wanting attention right away when her emotional needs for closeness were met.

When kids feel close to the people who care for them, they do not feel the need to act out in disturbing ways. This is because their need for attention is already met. Building a base of emotional availability can help a child feel less desperate, which can make them want to fight for attention that is not theirs.

It was different for each of my five kids to get attention. For example, Maya often wanted to be noticed for her own accomplishments among her successful brothers. If we did not acknowledge her accomplishments, whether they were at school or in family discussions, she would put on dramatic shows. Trivial things like asking her about her hobbies or taking the time to talk to her one-on-one about her goals helped her feel seen and heard, which I quickly learned. By making that link stronger, she no longer had to lie or act dramatic to get people's attention.

Being emotionally connected with our kids does not just mean spending time with them; it also means being aware of their emotional needs as they grow up. The truth is that kids who regularly feel emotionally supported are much less likely to act out in ways that get attention, because their basic emotional needs have already been met.

Developing emotional intelligence and encouraging healthy ways to talk about needs

It is possible that one of the most important things we can teach kids is how to understand and talk about their feelings in a healthy way. It has done wonderful things for both my patients and my kids. Once kids learn how to talk about or understand their feelings, they do not have to use manipulative or annoying behaviors to get what they want.

In one experience I had in the emergency room, an 8-year-old boy named James was often brought in after having a temper tantrum at home over something as silly as being told to turn off the TV or not getting a second serving of dessert. His mother was losing it because she did not know how to handle his temper tantrums. After making sure there were no major neurological or medical issues, we looked at the emotional triggers. James had a tough time figuring out how he felt and talking about it. Instead, he showed a lot of anger or rage.

I helped him get smarter about his feelings by working with his parents. James was told not to throw fits right away, but to say things like, "I feel frustrated" or "I am upset because..." James slowly started to get better after his parents gave him more ways to talk and told him that calm conversations were better than angry outbursts. It is powerful to teach kids how to name their feelings. If they can say something like, "I feel left out" or "I'm mad that you weren't listening," they are much less likely to act out to get attention, like having fits or crying a lot (Gottman, 2011).

It was a lot like this with my third son, Elai, when he was a teenager. As the middle child between Josh, who was still incredibly young, and her older brothers who were going to college, Elai sometimes felt like no one saw her. My wife and I taught him how important it was to say how he felt so he could say what he wanted to say without being passive-aggressive or annoying.

Rather than letting his anger build up when other people took over a family talk, we told Elai to say what he thought: "I'd like to share something too." Over time, Elai got much better at stating his needs, which stopped him from acting out or trying to get attention, which often happen when feelings are not expressed.

When parents, teachers, or health care professionals teach emotional intelligence, they give kids the words and tools they need to understand their own feelings. Emotional literacy, or being able to notice and name your feelings, can reduce behavior that is meant to get attention (Brackett, 2019). Children do not feel the need to act out when they know how to ask for attention in a healthy way.

Showing how to have healthy relationships and talk to people.

When we are parents, caregivers, or doctors, we forget how much kids watch us. Children will remember how we manage our own needs for attention, emotional expression, and speech for a long time as they learn how to interact with others.

Ethan was in his late teens when he came home one day clearly upset. He was upset with a close friend because he thought the friend was "overreacting" to something that was not clear. I sat down with him and tried to be calm. "Communicating effectively isn't just about what you say—it's about how you listen and communicate back," I said. When I worked on the hospital ward for a long time, I talked about how important it was to be patient and calm, especially when feelings were hurt. It was important to communicate clearly. We can build stronger relationships and get through misunderstandings with respect if we show others how to manage conflict by first validating their feelings, then talking about how to respond quietly, and finally stating our own needs without minimizing theirs.

I was shocked by how much this meant to Ethan. Over time, I saw him use the same approach with his own friends. It stopped being about "winning" emotional arguments and started being more about listening to others, being clear about his own needs, and calming down emotions before they got out of hand.

Children often behave in the same way as adults who argue or get angry, whether it is between parents or other adults in a confrontational situation (Scaramella et al., 2008). So, attention-seeking is not always a natural trait; it can also be caused by learned ways of interacting with others. A child will learn that emotional outbursts are the only way to get their needs met or their feelings accepted if they see people acting out to get the attention of a partner or coworker.

On the other hand, showing kids how to use calm conversation, empathy, and healthy emotional dialogue can help them use those skills themselves.

As a pediatrician, I try extremely hard to show others how to do this in the office. I always try to be cool when kids come in hurt or angry, and I want to interact with them in a way that does not reinforce unruly behavior or brush off their pain. This helps them understand that they can meet their needs without a lot of stress if they interact with adults or peers in a respectful and calm way.

Parents and teachers have the chance to show children how to be patient, empathetic, and understanding. This sets the tone for how kids learn to communicate respectfully.

Setting rules and expectations that are the same in all family or school settings.

When it comes to actions that are meant to get attention, consistency is key. Kids naturally push the limits to find out where they end. If these rules change based on the parent's mood or the location (like school vs. home), kids will keep changing their plan, which will usually make them want attention even more.

While I was helping a little girl named Lily in the emergency room one time, I saw how powerful inconsistent behavior could be. Lily, who was about nine years old, often had stomachaches that were not clearly caused by her body. It became clear after some in-depth conversations that Lily's home life was full of mixed hopes. Her parents were disorganized and had a lot on their plates with their jobs, so every day they had different standards for how she should behave. Some days they were flexible and willing to do what she asked, and other days they would snap in anger.

Without clear rules or consistent limits, Lily's attention-seeking through physical complaints got worse. Lily's symptoms did not start to get better until her parents got help setting clearer, more reliable limits for her behavior and how they would react to it.

For my third boy, Elai, a similar rule applied when it came to doing well in school. As the middle child, Elai sometimes felt like the rules of the house changed depending on where he stood in the family. Josh was the youngest, so some rules were less strict for him. Elai noticed right away. To fix this, my wife and I started holding regular family meetings and making sure that the rules and standards were clear for everyone, no matter what age. By making sure that standards were stable and fair, we helped Elai avoid feeling like he was being treated unfairly, which in turn stopped him from trying to get attention in quiet ways by comparing himself to others or rebelling quietly.

Kids naturally like to push the limits, but when rules are clear, consistent, and shared across all situations, like at home, at school, and in larger social groups, kids are less likely to act out in ways that are meant to get attention. By being completely consistent, kids and teens can build a keen sense of who they are.

In conclusion

Investing in strong emotional bonds, teaching emotional intelligence, setting a good example of healthy communication, and being clear about what is expected of kids are all long-term ways to stop them from doing bad attention-seeking behaviors. These tactics help kids build a strong emotional base so that they can become emotionally stable teens and young adults who do not have to use unhealthy habits to meet their emotional needs.

Being proactive is the best way for us as parents, caregivers, and medical experts to stop many of the attention-seeking behaviors we deal with. By building stronger emotional bonds, teaching them emotional literacy on a regular basis, and making sure our rules and how we talk to each other are the same in all settings, we give kids the stability, attention, and respect they want without having to be manipulated or interrupted.

When we show our kids how to behave and care for their feelings, we give them the best gift of all: the confidence and tools to manage their feelings in a healthy way.

References

Brackett, M. A. (2019). *Permission to Feel: Unlocking the Power of Emotions to Help Our Kids, Ourselves, and Our Society Thrive.* Celadon Books.

Gottman, J. M. (2011). *Raising an emotionally intelligent child: The heart of parenting.* Simon and Schuster.

Scaramella, L. V., Conger, R. D., & Simons, R. L. (2008). *Parental protective influences and the trajectory of delinquency.* Developmental Psychology, 44(6), 1674-1688.

Chapter 11

Encouraging Healthy Attention-Seeking Through Positive Reinforcement

----

During my practice, I have seen how kids' attention-seeking habits can range from loud and annoying to quiet and sincere. Lia, Ethan, Elai, Maya, and Josh are my five wonderful, strong-willed children. They have made me even more aware of how attention-seeking is not always a sad thing. In fact, all kids need attention—it is important for their growth. The important thing is to tell the difference between healthy and unhealthy ways of wanting attention and then use positive feedback to help them behave in a better way.

Promoting healthy attention-seeking means praising actions that help people become more independent, self-reliant, and emotionally mature. When kids feel like their needs for attention and connection are being met in ways that reward good behavior instead of unhealthy habits, they are less likely to throw tantrums, manipulate others, or do other sad things to get attention. This method has worked well for me in both my family life and my clinical job.

This chapter discusses how to change kids' attention-seeking from unhealthy to healthy by rewarding them for being independent, reinforcing good behavior, using praise and physical affection smartly, and using structured behavior modification tools like award systems and charts. These techniques can both stop and fix attention-seeking behaviors that might last all through childhood and puberty if they are not fixed.

Giving rewards for independence and noticing good behavior

My oldest daughter, Lia, graduated from college. It was a happy and sad time for me. As Lia became an adult, her need for attention changed. It went from wild emotional outbursts as a teenager to more subtle ways of wanting to be noticed for her achievements. One important thing I learned from Lia's teen years was how important it is to recognize independence.

The typical ways younger kids try to get their parents' attention do not work for bigger kids and teens who want to be independent. Instead, it looks like getting things done, solving problems, and making decisions, often without instant approval or supervision. For Lia, it meant working on a tough project herself, being smart about her college applications, and even being responsible in her social life.

However, just because bigger kids and teens do things independently, like Lia doing her first internship without us walking her through every step, does not mean they are not trying to get our attention. Yes, they are. They do not want someone to do things for them; instead, they want to be recognized for becoming more independent. People who care for kids need to learn how to praise this.

I would often take the time to talk to Lia after she had accomplished something big in her personal or academic life. I would tell her things like, "I'm so proud of how you managed that situation on your own" or "You're making decisions for yourself that show real strength of character." These compliments were not just empty words; they were meant to recognize competence and freedom and to stress how important it was to be able to rely on oneself.

In the same way, when I worked as a pediatrician, I saw how rewarding small steps toward freedom had a hugely positive impact on younger kids. Ellie was one of my patients. She was 9 years old and had a tough time making decisions because she always needed her parents to help her, like picking out her clothes in the morning or picking out a snack. Because they loved Ellie so much, her parents made her more dependent by giving her a lot of options and watching over things she could have done on her own.

I suggested that they start using positive feedback to reward Ellie for making choices on her own. Simple things like letting her pick out her own clothes for the week and then complimenting her choices helped her feel better about herself. Every time Ellie did something on her own, her parents made sure to tell her, "You did a great job picking that out by yourself!" Ellie's constant need for approval eventually went away as she became more confident in her own ability to make good choices.

Giving kids early rewards for being independent boosts their confidence. They learn that trying to do something on their own gets them good attention—attention that makes them feel more independent instead of lessening it. Children who are praised for good behavior are more likely to try to get attention from their parents in healthy ways instead of bad ones, like crying all the time, being spoiled, or asking for help with things they can do on their own (Kazdin & Rotella, 2021).

The Strength of Positive Attention, Verbal Praise, and Physical Touch

Jordan R. Chavez IV, M.D.

It is said that kids will do anything to be "caught being good." As a pediatrician and a parent, I have found this true. Verbal praise and love are two of the best ways to get kids to seek attention healthily. Teenagers and kids learn that they do not have to misbehave or lie to get attention if they are constantly praised for their good behavior.

Ethan is my second child and is now a medical student. When he was a teenager, speaking praise became especially important to him. Like his brothers, Ethan would sometimes do trivial things to show disobedience, especially when he felt low in self-esteem. I remember one day when he skipped a family get-together to stay home and study for the SAT. That night, he was grumpy while we celebrated Lia getting into college.

When I saw how badly Ethan wanted approval, I changed my plans. I did not scold Ethan for being alone; instead, I waited for him to do something good on his own. A few days later, after one of his study meetings, he told me that he had put his study materials together on his own and felt better prepared. I immediately saw this as a chance and praised his hard work: "Ethan, I saw how hard you've been working." That is great that you are really taking charge of your goals.

That one moment changed the way they talked to each other after that. After hearing praise, Ethan felt great about what he had accomplished, and it encouraged him to get attention by doing good things instead of pouting or pulling away. Verbal praise is not about complimenting kids on everything but building their self-esteem and letting them know you notice the good things about them. By praising Ethan for becoming more independent and determined, I stopped him from doing the kinds of sad things he might have done to get attention.

It is the same lesson when it comes to physical love. My youngest son, Josh, always liked a hug or a pat on the back to make him feel better. Even though recognition in words was helpful, physical touch showed him that he was seen and loved. When that love made him feel safe through touch, he did not have to act out to feel loved.

Giving young patients positive care, even in small ways, helped them a lot. A boy named Lucas was one of the kids I often worked with who would lie about small cuts or injuries to get attention. I did not brush off this behavior; instead, I praised him for being brave during his check-ups. I would tell him, "You are pretty brave; you did a great job getting through that." By focusing on his strength instead of how much he was lying, I saw his need to lie about his injuries go away.

Kazdin (2021) says children can healthily meet their emotional needs when they receive positive reinforcement at the right time. This can come in the form of words of support and loving actions. Kids are less likely to misbehave just to get your attention if you "catch" them doing something good and treat them with something good.

How to Change Unhealthy Behaviors into Healthy Need Expressions

When kids regularly act out in unhealthy ways to get attention, like whining, defiance, or exaggerating their physical complaints, the answer is not just to stop them but to teach them healthy ways to show what they need.

This idea produced Maya, the fourth child in our family known for having emotional outbursts from time to time. Maya was a strong person who did not mind telling everyone when she thought they were being unfair. However, she had to put on big shows because she could not always talk about her feelings in a way that made her feel heard or understood. Her over-the-top behavior was not helpful because she could not say what she needed, like love or attention. After all, she thought her brothers' accomplishments (often talked about more loudly in family conversations) were more important than hers.

Realizing this helped my wife and me help Maya talk about her feelings in better ways. We told Maya that instead of "throwing shade" at her boys or acting out at dinner when she felt unvalued, she should just say how she felt. The change was very noticeable. Maya learned that instead of acting out, she should say, "I worked hard on something, too, and I would like to share it." It did not happen right away, but these words replaced her more inappropriate body language over time.

As a pediatrician, I have helped young kids whose attention-seeking behavior was getting in the way of their lives make similar changes. Carolyn, a 7-year-old girl, comes to mind as a child who often messed up class by getting up during lessons. The teacher and parents were naturally mad, and they thought the behavior was just a sign of being restless. Carolyn was acting out, though, because she knew she needed to ask for help with her homework more directly but did not know how to say it helpfully.

I taught her how to ask for help when she was stuck with the help of her parents and teachers. By gently raising her hand, she could let us know that she needed extra help without having to get up and walk to the teacher's desk. Carolyn could do better in class after changing her more annoying attention-seeking behavior with this small, healthy way of expressing her needs.

Teaching kids how to say what they need is an important part of changing their unhealthy habits into healthy ones. Parents need to help their kids figure out what they want, like help, reassurance, or relief, and then show them how to ask for it correctly. This changes the emotional tools they have access to and stops them from using unhealthy reactions that try to get (but rarely get) the right attention (Barkley, 2020).

Behavior modification charts, reward systems, and other real-life examples

ATTENTION-SEEKING BEHAVIORS in CHILDREN

Although verbal praise and affection are suitable for kids' emotions, they sometimes need more organized and direct reinforcement to keep doing good things that get their attention. Tools for changing behavior, like charts and award systems, can work well here.

We found that a visual reward system worked well for Elai when he was about ten. Like many active kids his age, Elai sometimes had trouble asking for help in the right ways. Even when he knew we were busy with something else, he would knock on our bedroom door several times or ask the same question repeatedly. Even after much pleading and explaining, it was clear that giving directions aloud was not working. Simple reward coins, on the other hand, did work.

We gave Elai a token every time he politely and patiently asked for attention, help, or more information on a job. You could trade these tokens for small benefits like more screen time, a family movie night, or the choice of a dinner restaurant. Elai did very well in this method. Seeing instant, real-world rewards for his good behavior encouraged him to change his bad habit of interrupting others repeatedly with better ways to ask for attention.

I have told parents in the emergency room about similar techniques that they can use to help their kids who are acting out at school or at home to get attention. Sticking to school rules, staying seated during lessons, or doing chores without being asked are all good examples of behaviors that can be tracked on behavior modification charts. These charts help kids understand how to get positive attention.

For instance, a patient named Ethan, a boy with much energy, often acted up in class to get people to pay attention. After telling Ethan's parents and teacher about the prize system, we kept track of his progress by marking each day he met classroom behavior goals, like being quiet during reading time, raising his hand instead of yelling, etc. Over time, Ethan's unruly behavior improved over time because the visual chart and awards made it clear what behaviors were wanted.

Tools like behavior plans and reward systems can help maintain good habits. They give kids immediate feedback on their actions, reinforcing an effective way to get attention that does not involve unhealthy habits (Barkley, 2020).

In conclusion

Promoting healthy attention-seeking behaviors through positive feedback is one of the kindest and most effective ways to help kids healthily talk about their needs. By using verbal praise and affection to encourage independence, showing kids how to change destructive behaviors with healthy ways of expressing need, and giving them valuable tools like reward systems, we help them grow emotionally and gain confidence.

These well-thought-out methods give our kids and patients the tools they need to seek attention and affirmation in ways that boost their self-esteem and make them stronger emotionally. They learn that their needs are met not by being let down, but by talking to each other carefully, honestly, and respectfully. They stop having temper tantrums, complaining, or making over-the-top faces.

Seeking attention in a healthy way is the foundation for long-term mental growth. It changes kids' lives from one where they act out to get attention to one where they are bold about expressing their needs and those needs are met with love, support, and understanding.

References

Barkley, R. A. (2020). *18 Years of ADHD Experience: Transformation Case Histories*. The Guilford Press.

Kazdin, A. E., & Rotella, C. (2021). *The Kazdin Method for Parenting the Defiant Child: Without Pills, Therapy, or Breaking the Will*. Houghton Mifflin Harcourt.

Gottman, J. M. (2011). *Raising an Emotionally Intelligent Child: The Heart of Parenting*. Simon and Schuster.

Chapter 12

Teaching Children Self-Sufficiency and Confidence

One of the best things we can teach our kids is self-sufficiency. Being able to handle their own issues, decide what to do, and find their way around without help not only improves their skills but also boosts their confidence. By showing them that they can do well on their own, we help them build a sense of self-worth that does not depend on ongoing approval from others.

As a parent and as a worker in the emergency room, I have seen many times when kids feel lost when no one is telling them what to do. This could be because they are anxious, wanting attention, or just not having enough direction. But there is a fine line to walk: as parents and guardians, our job is to love and support our kids, but our main goal should not be to solve all their problems. Instead, we need to teach them how to deal with both successes and mistakes.

Jordan R. Chavez IV, M.D.

Here are some tips I have picked up at work and as a parent, along with stories and lessons on how to teach our kids to be independent and confident. We will talk about how to teach them how to deal with small problems, let them make their own choices, and help them develop a sense of self-worth that comes from inside themselves instead of outside sources.

Teaching kids how to handle small issues on their own.
One experience that comes to mind right away is taking care of a young boy named Kyle in the emergency room several times over the course of two years. Kyle often came in with small injuries like cuts, slightly swollen fingers, and even a splinter once. God bless her heart; his mom was worried about every little hurt and would rush to the emergency room for anything. Along the way, I became aware that Kyle, in turn, had almost no capacity for pain. Kyle would always want help right away, even if it was something as small as a paper cut. He would not even try to fix the problem himself.

One day, I talked to his mother alone. We talked about how Kyle could handle some of these small problems on his own. She said it was hard for her to see her child in any kind of pain, whether it was physical or mental. Still, we both agreed that letting him clean up his own cuts, put on bandages, or calm down before running to the emergency room might help him become stronger. The change was amazing when she started to use this method. Kyle went to the emergency room less often, and while he still got the occasional bump or bruise that comes with being a kid, he became much better at handling small problems on his own.

At home, I used the same approach with my kids, especially Maya, who, like many younger peers, had trouble controlling her impulses. Maya has become a strong young woman as she has grown up. She is now a girl majoring in finance, but when she was younger, she often asked others for help with things she could easily do herself. She would always ask her dad, "Dad, can you, do it?" when she was having trouble with something, like tying her shoes or opening a jar in the kitchen.

I stopped trying to solve every slight problem and started taking deliberate steps back. "Maya, why don't you give it a try first?" I'll help you if you really can't." In no time, this pattern paid off. She stopped automatically asking for help and started to believe in her own skills. Being able to do simple things on her own or figuring out how to solve a puzzle made her feel better about herself in more significant areas of her life. After some time, she produced her way of dealing with problems: try once, try again if that does not work, and only then ask for help or advice.

This idea is especially important for teaching kids how to be independent. We should not always solve their problems for them; instead, we should show them how to do it. We teach them that they are capable by putting them in situations where they must solve small problems, like school issues, home chores, or disagreements with other people. Over time, these small challenges make people stronger and more confident in their skills, which helps them in bigger parts of their lives.

Giving kids chances to make decisions and take charge of their own lives.

Giving kids the freedom to make their own choices is another important part of teaching them to be self-sufficient. This gives them the cognitive skills they need to think critically about their choices and the results of those decisions.

Ethan had an important event in his teenage years that changed his life. He is now a medical student. For one summer, he could choose between attending a sports camp or a science group. Ethan showed a lot of tension, even though his mother and I really wanted him to pick the workshop (we both really liked school), though. I thought of a key lesson I had learned about letting go of medical school: young people need to take responsibility for their choices, even if we do not agree with them completely. It helps them learn to be independent and take care of themselves. After telling him that he had to follow through with whatever choice he made, we let him make it.

Ethan picked the sports camp. While I quietly hoped he had become interested in science right away, letting him make the choice was the best thing we could have done for him. Ethan liked camp and did well with the leadership roles it offered. He also came back to school with a clearer head and ready to focus on his studies. For him, it was a substantial change. I could see him growing up and becoming responsible for his decisions, which is a good trait for him to have now that he is in medical school.

As a doctor, I see a lot of parents who, even though they mean well, make decisions for their kids. Lizzy is a 12-year-old kid who I have known since she was born, and I have seen her grow up. Amy, Lizzy's mother, tried to control every part of her daughter's life, from the things she did outside of school to the clothes she wore. Not in a helpful way, Lizzy was reacting and pushing back against Amy. During one appointment, I gently told Amy that it might be time to start letting Lizzy choose which things she wanted to focus on on her own. The idea was simple: instead of telling Lizzy what to do, let her choose between two or three choices.

Amy slowly gave Lizzy more freedom to make choices, and Lizzy reacted with more confidence. Giving Lizzy these chances showed her that her opinion was valued and, more importantly, that she could rely on her own judgment without being constantly watched.

Giving kids chances to make decisions on their own helps them become independent early on. Let little kids start. Letting a three-year-old choose what sweater to wear gives them a sense of power over their choices. As they get older, help them make bigger decisions, like what things to do outside of school, how to spend their weekly allowance, or what they are going to do on the weekend.

Autonomy does not mean that parents are no longer involved at all; it just means that we are more like guides than decision-makers. We help our kids think about the good and bad things about each choice, and then we trust them to make the best one for themselves. By going through this process, we are showing them that their choices and voices matter.

Helping kids build self-worth without relying on approval from others.

It is more important than ever to teach kids how to value themselves, especially in a world where social media and peer pressure make kids (and adults) want to get "likes," respect, and praise from other people. If kids always need other people to tell them they are smart or good enough, they will never learn the grit they need to deal with life's problems on their own.

In his early teens, Elai, my third child, had trouble with this. He was eager to keep up with his older brothers and always looked up to them, so he sometimes found himself going after praise. Whether it was big wins in school or small wins in sports, Elai was not motivated by the success itself. He was more interested in the praise he got from other people. He wanted other people to see how hard he was working and tell him he was doing an excellent job.

I knew right away that Elai needed help building up his own sense of self-worth instead of looking for approval from other people. I told him that instead of waiting for praise, he should value the process and get pleasure from hard work and personal growth. He started to change his mind slowly but surely. Elai stopped trying to get praise for everything he did and learned that it was more important to feel good about his own growth than to know if other people noticed.

Elai and some friends went hiking one weekend. When he got back, he did not brag about how far he had hiked or how high they had climbed, but there was a quiet happiness on his face. That was the first time I saw him truly proud of himself without wanting anyone to notice.

This lesson starts early and does not just apply to teens. We do not have to tell our kids "Good job!" or "You're amazing!" every time they do something good. Instead, we can ask them to think about how they feel about their efforts. "How do you think you did?" has always been one of my favorite things to ask my kids. This shows them that their own opinion of their work is more important than anyone else's (Deci & Ryan, 2000).

Children will gain from learning how to feel good about themselves without needing outside approval for a long time. When they find their own sense of self-worth, they will not have to look for approval everywhere, and they will not be as easily moved by social pressures or short-lived attention.

Ideas for activities: games, tasks, and creative outlets that help kids become more independent.

For kids, becoming independent should not be a boring and arduous process. It can and should be fun! Especially since I am raising five different kids, I have found that adding games and activities to daily routines helps kids become more independent and gives them the confidence to try new things. The following tasks were extremely helpful for both my family and some of the kids I have cared for in the emergency room.

1. Days of "Pick Your Own Adventure."
We loved the "Pick Your Own Adventure" days when Lia and Ethan were kids. We would let them plan our family trip every Saturday morning. They picked where we would go—the science center, the park, or the zoo. Because they got to pick what the day would be like, they felt like they had a say in family choices and were able to

take the lead. This can work for any family because it gives smaller kids a structured choice and gives older kids full freedom.

2. Making food and being responsible
"Cooking Nights" was another wonderful thing we did at home, especially with Elai and Maya. Every week, one of the kids would cook dinner for the family. Even when they were little, they loved having control in the kitchen (as long as they were watched, of course!). They would help pick recipes, do simple jobs like chopping veggies, or mix ingredients. It was more than just a meal; it was a whole lesson in taking responsibility and owning what you do. It did not matter if the food did not always taste five-star; the happy faces were worth it.

3. Chore charts with results
A simple job chart became a part of our daily life when Josh, my youngest child, started to push the limits a bit. Josh would get a sticker for every job he finished, like wiping the table or folding the laundry. When he reached a certain number of stickers, he could choose a prize like more playtime or family movie night. The catch was that parents could not help their kids with their work; they had to do it on their own. All our kids learned a lot about being responsible because of this.

4. Fun ways to boost your confidence
Finally, we made sure that all our kids had creative and independent tasks to help them feel proud of being themselves. Giving kids a creative outlet, like drawing and painting for Maya or making models for Ethan, helps them become more independent and motivated. When kids work on creative projects, they do not care what other people think. Instead, they focus on getting better at what they are doing and enjoying the happiness of making something on their own.

In conclusion

Teaching kids to be independent and confident is not just about getting them ready for life; it is also about making them strong, independent, and happy early on. We set children up to become confident, independent adults by helping them fix their own problems, giving them chances to make choices, giving them a sense of their own worth, and giving them fun things to do.

As parents, caregivers, and doctors, our main goal is to ensure that kids can do well on their own, encourage their curiosity, and teach them to trust themselves enough that they will not always need our approval or supervision. When kids understand that their own success, growth, and skills come from within, they are not only better prepared to deal with life's obstacles, but they also feel like they can make their own way from childhood to adulthood.

References

Deci, E. L., & Ryan, R. M. (2000). *Self-determination theory and the facilitation of intrinsic motivation, social development, and well-being.* American Psychologist, 55(1), 68-78.

Kazdin, A. E., & Rotella, C. (2021). *The Kazdin Method for Parenting the Defiant Child: Without Pills, Therapy, or Breaking the Will.* Houghton Mifflin Harcourt.

Ryan, R. M., & Deci, E. L. (2017). *Self-determination theory: Basic psychological needs in motivation, development, and wellness.* Guilford Press.

Chapter 13

The Role of Educators and School Environments in Addressing Attention-Seeking

----

As a doctor and a father of five, it has been clear to me for a long time that talking about a child's emotional and behavioral needs means more than just talking about them at home. A lot of a child's formative years are spent in school, and the setting inside those walls has a significant impact on how their behaviors, especially wanting attention, are understood, dealt with, and eventually changed.

I remember the change very well. My second son Ethan had trouble with attention-seeking habits when he was younger. Ethan was always smart, but his excitement would sometimes show up suddenly and in a big way. He would talk over his first-grade teacher in the middle of a lesson, cause problems in the classroom, and often act like the class clown to keep everyone's attention on him. I knew about this behavior at home, and we worked to change it, but the problem got worse at school. During a meeting with his parents, his teacher got angry and said, "He's smart, but he's always trying to get attention." Things are getting too bad.

At that time, I realized that while I was helping Ethan deal with his feelings at home, the school setting did not have the right tools to help him. I knew that collaborating with the school could make a significant difference, but teachers also needed to understand that attention-seeking actions were not just "bad behavior"; they were signs that the child's emotional needs were not being met.

The complex but key role schools play in forming children's emotional landscapes will be discussed in this chapter, with a focus on how parents and teachers can work together. We will talk about ways teachers can recognize attention-seeking as a sign of need, classroom-based behavioral interventions, and how important it is to create welcoming schools where students can use group activities and relationships with peers as healthy ways to deal with their feelings.

Methods of working together between home and school

In all the years I have worked in the emergency room, I have seen many parents come in to get help because they were afraid about their child's unruly behavior at school. Many parents have said, "He's a whole different kid at home!" because they are upset about stories of attention-seeking behavior in the classroom. Many kids have this problem because they feel like the rules at home are different from the rules at school, even though school is usually more organized.

When Ethan's behavior in class went beyond being a nuisance, my wife and I collaborated closely with his teacher to solve the problem. We began to write down trends of his behavior in both home and school settings, paying special attention to times when he seemed to act out the most. It became clear that Ethan needed more attention when he was scared or uncertain, which is something I had not fully talked about when we only worked on schoolwork at home.

When Ethan's teacher and I produced a plan for positive attention, we made progress. His teacher agreed to give him "leadership" jobs, which were small roles like handing out worksheets or helping set up lesson materials. These gave him a structured way to meet his need to be involved. At the same time, we pushed him even more at home, letting him know that these times of duty at school were just as important to us as how well he did in school.

Ethan's mental needs were met on both fronts by home and schoolworking together. He did not have to stress about trying to prove himself or "perform" for attention. He stopped having to be the class clown to feel like he was seen; he learned how to use his energy in an effective way.

When working with young people, the same way of thinking applies. I once saw a boy named Ethan whose parents were dealing with reports from school that he had frequent meltdowns. After visiting the school to get a better sense of how it works and talking to teachers, it was clear that Ethan felt stressed during unplanned times like free play and the time between lessons. His teacher was able to change the routine of the classroom by adding more specific times for led play and shorter times for transitions. At home, Ethan's parents worked with the same basic idea: order lowered the stress that made Ethan act out to get attention.

Using collaborative methods is especially important for dealing with these habits. Communication between teachers, parents, and school counselors makes sure that methods work the same way at home and at school, which are the two most important places for kids to learn outside of playtime (DuPaul & Stoner, 2014).

Getting teachers to see attention-seeking as a need instead of a bad habit

There is a significant difference between thinking that a child's temper tantrum is unruly behavior and seeing it as them expressing emotional needs that are not being met. The first one usually leads to punishment in the classroom, while the second one asks for help and understanding. Teachers can better handle attention-seeking behaviors when they see them as cries for help or attempts to be noticed instead of interruptions.

Maya, my fourth child, has always been good at acting. It showed when she first started school. She was not openly rebellious, but when her feelings got strong, they would show in ways that could sometimes mess up the class. Mrs. Miller, Maya's third-grade teacher, was very patient with her because she knew that Maya's temper tantrums got worse when she did not feel like she was a part of class discussions, especially when her older boys' good grades came up at parent-teacher conferences. Mrs. Miller told us that Maya's face would light up when she felt like she was contributing and that she would calm down quickly when she was given a job or role that made her responsible.

We worked to make Maya understand that she did not have to make her acts more dramatic to be seen. Mrs. Miller is one of the best teachers because she did not punish Maya for trying too hard to stand out. Instead, she helped her turn her wants into good things. Mrs. Miller was right when she thought Maya's behavior was more about wanting attention than being rebellious. She noticed that Maya became more involved in class when she was given leadership roles or asked to share projects that were important to her.

Teachers and counselors who are good at their jobs know how to change "bad behavior" in the classroom into emotional expression. Students are more patient with teachers who make this change, and teachers who make this change are also good at stopping fights before they get worse. The important thing is to realize that every urge to act out is a need—a need to be seen, to feel in charge, or to say things you have not said yet.

I have often told parents that it is also their job to help teachers understand that attention-seeking is not always something that needs to be stifled or pushed down. Instead, teachers should act like detectives and look for patterns in their students' behavior. They should also know when a child is asking for more than just a time-out or "redirection."

When kids' unruly behavior is seen with kindness, they feel like their needs are being met, and they are not as likely to act out to get what every kid wants: approval, attention, and care (Greene, 2016).

Redirecting, time-outs, and affirmations are all behavior interventions that can be used in the classroom.

Structured behavioral interventions are especially important for changing unhealthy habits, especially in a school with many kids trying to get the same attention. Compassion and understanding are especially important when dealing with attention-seeking behavior. It can be tricky to ensure that interventions do not encourage the behavior you want to stop.

Redirecting is a popular method I have often told teachers to use. Let us look at Elai when he was in the first few years of school. He never caused a fuss, but there were times when he could not stop thinking about trivial things, like raising his hand repeatedly even though he did not have anything new to say. His teacher quietly started to steer him toward other tasks that made sense to her. She stopped always answering his raised hand, which made him angry when she did not call on him. Instead, she started offering other things to do or asking him to help a friend with their work. This way,

Elai could feel like he was contributing and was important without taking over the class's attention.

Redirection works because it helps kids reach their goal (which is to feel like they are contributing or important) without encouraging unruly behavior.

The smart use of time-outs is another measure that has worked well in the classroom. Time-outs should never be used as a punishment. Instead, they should be used to give the child a chance to calm down. I remember a case involving Bryce, a young boy whose parents came to me because other kids were complaining about how he was acting out during reading time. Instead of giving him consequences right away, Bryce's teacher used planned timeouts that gave him a chance to calm down. Bryce was able to sit in a calm place for a few minutes, get his bearings, and then go back to the group. This time-out was not a "punishment corner." It was just a place for Bryce to calm down before getting back to work.

For some patients, I suggested classroom mantras, which are helpful, especially for kids who are already low on confidence. One case that stands out is with a girl named Lily, who came to see me a lot because she got headaches during hard math classes for no apparent reason. Once I knew that math was what set her off, I suggested that her teacher use encouragement ahead of time, telling Lily things like "I believe in you" or "You've got this" before the lesson even started. This slight change in the way they talked had a big effect: Lily's "headaches" went away, and she learned to connect math with success instead of failure. The mantras gave her positive emotions, which stopped her from acting out to get attention by complaining about her symptoms all the time.

It is important that behavioral treatments do not feel too good or too bad. Redirecting their attention, time-outs, and positive reinforcement are all gentle ways to help them learn better ways to handle attention. When you add care for the emotional needs that are at the root of the problem, it makes all the difference.

What's Important About Group Activities, Peer Discussions, and Policies That Include Everyone at School

Attention-seeking habits are often encouraged by the way schools are set up, with their focus on individual success or competition. When students always feel like they need to do better than their peers, they might do anything to stand out. Focusing on group activities and inclusive school rules that encourage connection over competition can make this dynamic a lot less harmful.

For instance, Maya did very well in tasks were working together was valued more than individual success. She often felt like she had to do well in fourth grade, not just for herself but also to keep up with her brothers Ethan and Elai. Maya did not feel more at ease in class until her teacher added more group tasks. She could work with others and make a difference when she worked on projects with a group, where the result was more important than her work. This made her feel less like she had to prove herself all the time, which made her less likely to put on big shows to get attention.

School activities with other kids help them feel like they belong, not because they are the loudest or most noticeable, but because they make a real difference in the lives of their peers. This change has happened most smoothly in schools where everyone is welcome, and teamwork, group work, and peer discussions are valued.

I remember being a consultant for a school that used peer talks to instruct students about emotional literacy. A program called "Classroom Circles" was created so students could talk about their thoughts in a safe group setting. This open-minded method kept kids socially active and made classrooms where kids could understand and share each other's feelings and points of view. Students who used to shout and yell to get attention learned that they could be heard if they were quiet and participated in talks that focused on mutual respect instead of angry outbursts.

This part of being inclusive should go beyond just group events or discussion times; it should also be a part of the school's overall rules. Children who might otherwise feel left out or ignored can benefit from programs that value diversity and honor different learning styles. This means that students do not have to act out to get attention.

In conclusion

One of the most important places for shaping how kids deal with and share their emotional needs is at school, especially when those needs are attention-seeking behaviors. We do not have to see these actions as problems; instead, we can work together at home and school to make understanding and compassion a part of everyday life. When teachers see attention-seeking as an emotional need instead of unruly behavior, they can help kids learn to control their emotions better using controlled methods like time-outs and redirection. At the same time, group games and discussions with other students that promote inclusivity in the classroom help kids express themselves healthily, lowering their need for constant approval from others.

If everyone works together—teachers, parents, counselors, and students—we can create home and school settings that are good for emotional health. This partnership between institutions and families helps kids learn how to balance their need for attention with the skills they need to handle themselves, become more self-aware, and build their confidence.

References

DuPaul, G. J., & Stoner, G. (2014). *ADHD in the Schools: Assessment and Intervention Strategies*. Guilford Press.

Greene, R. W. (2016). *Lost and Found: Helping Behaviorally Challenging Students (and, While You are at It, All the Others)*. Wiley.

Kazdin, A. E. (2021). *The Kazdin Method for Parenting the Defiant Child: With No Pills, No Therapy, No Contest of Wills.* Houghton Mifflin Harcourt.

Jordan R. Chavez IV, M.D.

Chapter 14

Parental Self-Care and Emotional Balance

I have personally seen how stress and emotional burnout can affect both patients and the people who care for them. I have had more than my fair share of sleepless nights, hard conversations, and times of reflection while raising my five kids with my loving wife. Their names are Lia, Ethan, Elai, Maya, and Josh. In these times, I learned something significant: as a parent, taking care of yourself is just as important as taking care of your kids.

To some, the idea that putting your health first as a parent can make you a better caregiver may seem strange, but this is precisely what I have seen and heard from families I have helped over the years. Being a parent is both satisfying and stressful at times. If we do not take care of our mental health, it affects not only our own lives but also the lives of our children.

This chapter discusses the importance of parents taking care of themselves and how stress, exhaustion, and emotional burnout can change how we respond to our kids' attention-seeking behaviors. We will also discuss how to be thoughtful parents, control ourselves, and build support networks so that as parents, we can take care of our own needs first.

Why it is important to take care of your emotional health as a parent.

You cannot pour from an empty cup. This is one of the most important things I have learned as a father and pediatrician. This became noticeably clear when our third child, Elai, was born. Our oldest child, Lia, was getting ready to start middle school. On the other hand, Ethan was becoming more active, interested in everything, and always wanted attention. It was easy for me to forget about something important: my mental health, as I tried to make sure our first two kids went to soccer practices, read for school, and tied their shoes.

When our baby Elai came home, my wife and I were worn out. I still worked long hours in the emergency room, and she was taking care of herself, the house, and the family. There were days when everything seemed too much. The baby's crying seemed like another thing that was getting in the way of a good night's sleep, and I felt like I was losing my patience. It hit me: Parenting burnout is not just an idea but absolute. I sometimes lost it, and it was not just with my kids. It happens slowly but leaves clear marks on how we deal with our kids' mental needs.

It takes much mental strength to raise kids, and those strengths can run out if we do not take care of our own needs, too. This is easy to forget, mainly if you are focused on giving your child everything they need. This has also happened to some parents I have worked with in the emergency room. One case that stands out is Grace, a mother who often took her young, noisy son Ethan to the emergency room. He liked to act out, and he would often say that he had minor injuries like scrapes or leg pain that were not there. At first, I noticed how upset and angry Grace looked every time we saw her. It seemed like every time her son yelled, it added to the stress she was already feeling.

I asked Grace how she was doing in a soft voice after her third visit in two months. Sometimes, clinicians forget to ask this question because they are so focused on their patients that they forget that the people taking care of them are also people. She sighed and told me about her long workday, her sick mother who lived in a different state, and how hard it was for her to keep Ethan from acting out without losing her cool. I could tell Grace was mentally worn out, not just from Ethan's behavior. She had been carrying too many things without any breaks.

Parents often think that taking a break, asking for help, or even saying they are tired is a sign of failing or being selfish. However, it is important to remember that taking care of your mental health gives your kids the stability they need. When you are mentally stable and balanced, your kids' attention-seeking behaviors do not seem like big problems but somewhat manageable chances to connect with them. Being aware of yourself is not a form of self-indulgence; it is how you make sure you can help the people who need you the most (Rutherford, Wallace, Laurent, & Mayes, 2015).

How stress, fatigue, and emotional burnout can change how you react to your child's behavior.

From my experience as both a doctor and a parent, I can say with certainty that how parents react to their kids often shows how they feel inside. How physically and emotionally worn out we are directly affects our tendency to snap, get angry, or stop caring.

I saw this happen during my son Ethan's busy middle school years. Although he was naturally interested and loved to ask questions, his need for attention sometimes wore me down, especially after a long shift in the emergency room. I remember a day when I worked two 12-hour shifts in a row. When I got home, all I wanted was some quiet time. However, Ethan, who was overly excited, ran into the living room and started pulling on my shirt as he tried to tell me about a fight with a friend at school.

Sometimes, I can't wait to hear what someone has to say, but that day, every word he said was like throwing a rock into a pond that was already rough. I lost it. "Ethan, do not do that now!" I felt terrible about it right away. I could tell from the look on his face that what he needed at that moment was not my anger but my understanding. But if you are already terribly busy and a small action feels like it could make things worse, it is time to take a step back and do something nice for yourself.

Being stressed, tired, or burned out significantly changes how we interact with our children. Because we are tired or stressed, we tend to see attention-seeking not as a sign that "I need you" but as noise—annoying noise. When parents respond this way, it significantly affects how kids think about their actions. When kids constantly ask for attention and are met with anger or disinterest—which can happen because parents are stressed—it makes them angrier and may make them act worse (Petersen, Joseph, & Feit, 2014).

It is important to remember that our kids watch us and learn how to deal with their stress and feelings. If we react to their actions by getting angry or pulling away, they learn that that is an effective way to deal with stress. We can teach others how to communicate well and understand their emotions by showing them how to control their own by recognizing their needs. For example, instead of snapping at Ethan, we could say, "I love hearing about your day, but I need a moment to rest and gather myself first."

During my meetings with parents, I have seen this process of reflection happen. After one of our talks, a mother once told me, "I see it now..." "He is much less patient when I am mad. It was not him; it was us both." Even though this knowledge is subtle, it has much power to break cycles of emotional burnout.

Being a mindful parent and showing kids how to control themselves

I did not always use the word "mindful parenting" when I first started raising my kids, but now I see that it is what I have been trying to do at work and home. Mindful parenting involves being present, both physically and emotionally, and staying aware of your needs, your feelings, and your child's needs.

When my five younger children were together, things were sometimes crazy, and I often felt bad that I could not meet everyone's needs. Coming home one winter, I remember Maya, who was five years old, having a temper tantrum over a broken toy. Elai was already angry because he and Ethan fought about screen time limits, and Lia went back and forth between them to try to calm things down. When I got home, it was a mess because I had just ended a hard case at the emergency room.

There was a strong urge to explode and scream, "Just stop!" because I was stressed out. However, something stopped me. At that very moment, I took a big breath. I am unsure if it was because I was tired or if my mind suddenly became more apparent. I did not get mad or upset. Instead, I sat still in the middle of the family room for five minutes. They did not stop right away, but they did look. The younger kids slowly noticed that I was calm and came together. I finally got Maya to sit on my lap, and Elai started talking. He was not talking about their toy war but about how upset he was when things were unfair.

In this peaceful and aware moment, I realized I had shown someone something constructive: how to control themselves. My kids learned a unique way to deal with their feelings when they saw me not responding to chaos with more chaos right away. I taught them to stop, breathe, and gather themselves before replying.

Being a mindful parent means realizing that you do not have to step in or control every situation right away. Mindfulness, on the other hand, tells parents to be calm in all conditions. In turn, children pick up this sense of order. Over time, they learn to stop, think about their actions, and not react emotionally immediately (Kabat-Zinn & Kabat-Zinn, 2014).

Being a mindful parent helps you understand and care for yourself and your child. It helps you remember that you are only human and that taking breaks, being kind to yourself, and recharging are all important parts of being a good parent.

Support Systems for Parents: When to Ask Family, Friends, and Professionals for Help

As a parent, one of the hardest things for me to accept was that I could not do everything—at least not by myself. You are not a loser just because you say you need help. There is no better way to show yourself and your kids how strong you are than to do this.

My wife and I knew early on that we needed help because we had five kids. Grandparents, uncles, and close family friends were extremely helpful to us, especially when I was in the middle of medical training or when my wife was busy at work. It felt like breathing when someone stepped in to give us a break.

A specific Thanksgiving is one I will never forget. Ethan and Elai were getting into a bigger fight than usual. It was time for Lia to hang out with her friends, and Maya had just started constantly whining, which none of us could handle. We asked my sister-in-law for help at the last minute of that holiday, and she kindly offered to watch the kids for the afternoon. After several hours, my wife and I went for our first walk in months without stopping. That short break made us feel like we had been on holiday for a month, and when we got back, we were full of energy.

In my work with kids, I have often told their parents that they should get help from a professional. Just like we go to friends for a break or some happy encouragement now and then, there are times when we need to talk to a counselor, therapist, or parent support group. Going to therapy is not a sign of weakness, especially if you are dealing with burnout, mental exhaustion, or acting out. Working with a mental health worker can help some parents learn new ways to deal with their own and their child's emotions and build emotional strength for everyone (Peterson & Bush, 2020).

Support systems are important for keeping your mental balance and being a good parent. You can talk to a family member about how stressed you are, share your problems with friends, or get professional help. No one expects you to be perfect, but being around people who can give you different points of view will help you manage the good and bad aspects of being a parent.

In conclusion

Raising them is both mentally challenging and rewarding, no matter how many kids you have. And being able to take care of yourself is a key part of being a good, caring, and loving parent. If you want to manage attention-seeking habits with balance and grace, the old saying "putting on your oxygen mask first" hits home.

By taking care of your emotional health, slowing down, learning emotional regulation through mindfulness, and getting help when you need it, you can make your home a more calm, caring, and active place. Your kids learn from you how to deal with problems and stress with kindness instead of anger, and you give them one of the most important gifts of all: the power to control themselves.

It takes much work to be a parent, and you must ensure you take care of yourself. Self-care does not mean you have to be perfect; it just means being there for yourself and your kids as you go through life's many changes.

References

Kabat-Zinn, M., & Kabat-Zinn, J. (2014). *Everyday Blessings: The Inner Work of Mindful Parenting.* Hachette Books.

Petersen, A. J., Joseph, K. L., & Feit, M. D. (2014). *Parenting and stress: understanding experiences, contexts, and consequences.* In Parenting Matters: Supporting Parents of Children Ages 0-8 (pp. 250-271). National Academies Press (US).

Peterson, C. M., & Bush, K. (2020). *Parenting with Insights from American Family Studies: An Overview.* Routledge.

Rutherford, H. J. V., Wallace, N. S., Laurent, H. K., & Mayes, L. C. (2015). *Emotional Experience and Parenting: When Emotion Coaching and Emotion Dismissing Interact with Maternal Stress.* Developmental Psychology, 51(4), 572–581. https://doi.org/10.1037/a0038545

Jordan R. Chavez IV, M.D.

Chapter 15

Transforming Attention-Seeking into Constructive and Trusting Relationships

----

As a father of five—the always-curious Lia, the studious Ethan, the ambitious Elai, the Maya, and the ever-inquisitive Josh—and as a doctor, most of that time in the stressful environment of an emergency room, I've learned to see attention-seeking behaviors not as a bothersome thing, but as a clear and human need to connect. It is easy to get annoyed when your child acts up because they want your attention, especially when you are already stressed out from everyday life. But as I have worked as a therapist and raised my own kids, it has become clear to me that attention-seeking is not about getting extra attention; it is about showing a basic need for approval, love, and safety.

I want parents and other adults who care for kids to look at attention-seeking with wonder and empathy instead of anger or impatience. How we react to these cries from our kids can either keep the fights and misunderstandings going or help them build relationships based on trust that will benefit their long-term mental health. This chapter will talk about how encouraging connection instead of ignoring attention-seeking can turn difficult habits into chances for growth, family unity, and bonding.

Seeing attention-seeking to connect with others instead of a bothersome behavior

When parents come into my office, they are usually incredibly angry and ask things like, "Why is she acting out?" or "Why doesn't he just listen instead of becoming angry to get my attention?" Most of the time, they feel worn out and like the only reason for their behavior is rebellion or manipulation. While sometimes kids act out just because they can, most of the time it is because they need to connect with others and feel like they are important.

When my second son Ethan was four years old is a noticeably clear case that comes to mind. He was a remarkable child even at that age—keenly watchful and intellectually curious. As the demands of my medical school training got tougher, though, I found myself mentally pulling away. As I looked over my hospital notes one evening in the living room, Ethan tried to show me something—a Lego building he had made—but I was too busy with my work to pay attention. Not long after that, Ethan got mad and ran upstairs, only to come back and quickly throw the Legos on the floor in front of me. At first, I wanted to tell him off for making a mess, but I stopped myself. Is there more to this than this? Was this act of rebellion just a way for me to take my mind off my work for a moment?

Ethan told me that he wanted me to play with him but did not think I cared about what he was making during a simple chat. There was more to his Legos than just toys. He was building a way for me to enter his world again.

When Ethan or any of my other kids did something to get my attention, that moment changed how I dealt with it. When one of them acted out, I started to ask myself, "What is the message here?"

I was able to change how I felt about attention-seeking by seeing it as a call for connection instead of an act of rejection. I went from being angry or frustrated to being interested, curious, and involved.

I have worked with kids like Maya, who was seven years old and would often break down in tears when her mom came to pick her up from school, especially if the day seemed to go on for too long. At first, her mother thought these outbursts of feeling were too much or too dramatic. But after talking to her, we found out that Maya was having a tough time with the long times she was not with her mother. She was not acting out to make a scene; she was acting out because she needed to feel safe as she went from school to home.

Once Maya's mother realized that she was trying to connect with her, she changed how she dealt with her. Before school, she gave her more mental support, throughout the day she sent her short messages to check in, and after school, they changed their schedule to spend more time together. Maya's temper tantrums happened much less often after these simple changes because her emotional needs were met before her behavior got worse.

A lot of the time, parents think their kids are trying to "push buttons," but most of the time, kids are just trying to connect with others. We have a much better chance of replacing disruptive behaviors with trust, open communication, and safety if we take the time to notice and meet this natural need to connect with others (Gordon, 2000).

Taking care of a child's long-term emotional health by meeting their needs for approval, love, and stability

To raise a child who is emotionally healthy, we must first meet their wants for approval, love, and peace of mind. The fact that a child acts out repeatedly to get attention means that they do not know if their needs are being met. As parents and teachers, our job is to make sure they know that they are important in a clear and consistent way.

I think about my oldest daughter, Lia, and how hard it was for my wife and me to keep everything in check when she became a teenager. Lia people have always been very independent. But there were times in high school when she tried to get attention by having long arguments about what was fair or by following extremely strict routines. And sometimes our first thought was that this was just the stubbornness of being a teenager. But as we dug deeper, we saw that Lia was trying to get attention because she needed to feel validated. I do not think she was evaluating us just for fun. She was trying to figure out who she was in a world that was changing so quickly. She was not trying to argue with us; she was trying to talk about her ideas with the people she trusted the most and be sure that we would agree with her during that important stage of growth.

To meet that need, I made sure to validate her feelings even when we did not agree. I also reminded her that our love for her was not based on her agreeing with us; it was based on having honest talks. That one time we had a very intense argument about curfew, I told her, "I want you to know that I see how hard you're working to balance respect and independence." What you say shows that you gave it some thought, which I respect. It was not about winning the fight; it was about recognizing her effort, her thought, and her desire to connect.

As a pediatrician, I often talk to parents about this issue. To meet a child's need for validation, you do not have to give in to their requests. Instead, you should acknowledge their feelings and show them that your point of view is important. Validation helps kids understand that their feelings are important, which in turn makes them stronger emotionally.

Take Henry, a nine-year-old boy whose parents often brought him to my office because he was acting up at school. After trying different approaches and interventions, I learned Henry's home life was not stable. It was not that his parents were not caring, but recent events like a move, financial stress, and changes in the family dynamic had made it an emotionally unstable place for him. Henry was angry not to cause trouble but because he needed to know that his family would still love and support him through all these changes.

As soon as his parents realized this, they worked to set up stricter routines and clear, reliable rules. Spending more valuable time with Henry and making sure he had regular check-ins made an enormous difference in both his behavior at school and his emotional state. Henry needed security, and the consistency his parents built into his life gave him the support he needed for his mental health to improve.

Kids' emotions are complicated, and behaviors that try to get our attention are often caused by unmet wants for love, approval, and consistency. Not only do these things make relationships healthier, but they also teach kids to trust that their mental health is important to their family (Siegel & Bryson, 2020).

Transforming difficult behaviors into chances to connect and grow

When we change how we think about our kids' actions and see them as chances to connect with them, we see them for what they really are: chances to teach, build trust, and grow with them. Every outburst, tantrum, or act of defiance teaches both the parent and the kid something important.

I remember that one summer when Ethan was a teenager, his anger showed up in some behavior problems. They were not too bad, but they were bad enough that we had to have regular tough talks. We were going to build a bench for the backyard one day together. This was a project we were both excited about at first. But after ten minutes, Ethan's mood changed. He stormed off, angry that the measures were wrong.

At first, I was angry and wanted to finish the job by myself. However, I had a feeling that this was not just about the bench. Ethan needed to be reassured and shown that mistakes are normal, and they can be used to improve. I gave him some time and then went up to him later, not angry but with an offer: "How about we work this out together?"

That moment was not just about straightening up a board or nail that was in the wrong place; it was about dealing with anger, making room for growth, and showing that our relationship could manage tough times. By having Ethan help me "fix" the mistake, I showed him that problems could be turned into chances to learn, without feeling bad or guilty.

In the emergency room, I see a lot of cases where kids' behavior is just seen as a problem. Lucy, an 11-year-old girl, stood out as a patient because she was always cranky during her many trips. Her mother would often roll her eyes because she thought Lucy's complaining was not necessary or was not true. But on one visit, I took a few extra minutes to talk to Lucy directly. We talked about things other than her health problems.

Lucy's irritable behavior was a cover for her nervousness. She was tense because of changes in her family, and every visit made her feel like a "problem" instead of a person. The way they talked to each other changed after I told her mother this. Lucy's mother began to include her more in decisions about her care and asked for her opinion instead of ignoring it. That one simple action changed Lucy's behavior from disconnection to involvement. She stopped complaining all the time because she felt like she was being heard.

We can show care, learn, and work together when we do not see behavioral problems as things that need to be fixed but as ways to understand each other better. We allow stronger bonds to form, trust to grow, and for both parents and kids to understand that tough times are a normal part of any good relationship.

Finally, I want to stress the importance of empathy, patience, and the fact that parents are always learning.

Like life itself, being a parent is a journey of learning, change, and growth that never ends. People often see attention-seeking behaviors as annoying problems that need to be "fixed." But these behaviors can also be great chances to connect with our kids on a deeper level, learn to understand how to show empathy, and realize that sometimes the smallest pleas for help have the deepest roots.

As a dad, the journey with Lia, Ethan, Elai, Maya, and Josh had many times when my patience and ability to understand were put to the test. But with each year and each struggle, I have learned that patience and understanding are the most important parts of any good relationship.

We need to remember ourselves that nothing stays the same, whether we are calming a toddler down after a temper tantrum or listening to a teen's worries. Our children are always changing, and so should we. There is not a set way to go through this—every moment of parenting will be different, just like every kid is different.

When we really understand what empathy means, we are there for our kids, both when they are happy and when they are trying hard to get our attention. We can turn these moments into lasting ties that will be passed down from one generation to the next by reacting with love, acceptance, and patience.

Here is one last thought for you, dear reader: We are not perfect parents. We are growing up with our kids. Every time someone does something that bothers us, we ask ourselves, "How can we use this moment to strengthen our connection?" When we feel empathy, we turn attention-seeking into trust. Being patient helps people understand each other. And love is how we help our kids grow, both mentally and in other ways.

References

Gordon, T. (2000). *Parent Effectiveness Training: The Proven Program for Raising Responsible Children.* Three Rivers Press.

Siegel, D. J., & Bryson, T. P. (2020). *The Power of Showing Up: How Parental Presence Shapes Who Our Kids Become and How Their Brains Get Wired.* Ballantine Books.

Jordan R. Chavez IV, M.D.

Conclusion

A Framework for Lifelong Empowerment

The emergency room is a busy and emotional place. I have learned that attention-seeking habits are a normal and even necessary part of growing up. As a dad to five kids—Lia, Ethan, Elai, Maya, and Josh—I know personally how hard and how rewarding it can be to figure out what a child wants when they are begging for our attention.

In these last few thoughts, I want to put together everything that being a parent and a doctor has taught me about habits that try to get attention. We have been on a trip through this book that turns attention-seeking from a behavior that parents often find annoying into a way to learn more about what a child needs. This change helps us build safe relationships, grow emotionally, and stay strong throughout our lives. As parents or guardians, it is our job to help, listen, and turn even the strangest behaviors into chances for growth and connection, from birth through youth and beyond.

We have talked about the most important ways to deal with and change attention-seeking behaviors. We have also looked at how these strategies change as a child grows up. Finally, we have talked in depth about how love, clear expectations, and communication can help our kids do well. As we come to the end of this trip, let us go over these main ideas one more time and think about how they can help us become more powerful throughout our lives.

Putting together a list of important strategies for dealing with and changing attention-seeking behaviors

I have helped worried parents and frustrated guardians for decades, and I have seen how understanding can change things. We need to stop seeing attention-seeking as just annoying, problematic, or manipulative behavior. This is one of the most significant changes we have talked about. We now see it for what it really is: a deep need for love, relationship, and approval.

Maya, my fourth child, was very outspoken and would not keep it to herself when she felt pushed aside or ignored. She was not acting out or defiant when she stormed off after a fight with her bigger brothers or made loud requests for praise for her accomplishments. She was just trying to get attention. It was more of a question: "Do you see me?" "Do you care about me?"

Not to stop or silence these behaviors was not the answer for Maya or many other kids like her. Instead, they needed to learn how to react with empathy, validation, and limits. When we met Maya's needs by recognizing real moments of connection—through conversations, praise when it was due, and chances to do things together—her over-the-top attempts to get our attention changed into more subdued, confident ones.

Just as much, this rule applies to my patients. Parents often complain in the emergency room, not only about their kids' behavior problems but also about how frustrating it is that they have tried so many "discipline" methods that do not work. The truth is that we will always be on a reactive loop if we do not look at attention-seeking behavior without considering the child's unmet emotional needs. We can directly meet those needs by using techniques like active listening, positive reinforcement, and shared problem-solving (Calkins & Leerkes, 2011). This makes less room for the behavior's more negative parts.

The following is what we now know about key strategies:

- Reframe attention-seeking as a desire for relationship instead of defiance.
- As kids grow and progress, you should meet them where they are.
- Set clear but fluid limits and change how we react so that we show understanding instead of punishment.
- Make sure kids know they are seen and heard, even when they are acting badly, by validating their feelings before "correcting" them.
- Instead of focusing only on bad behaviors, use positive feedback that highlights effort and healthy expression.

In the end, these strategies reinforce ideals that help people be emotionally intelligent and strong for life. We help our kids learn how to deal with their feelings in healthy and satisfying ways by getting to the root of attention-seeking—through connection, advice, and validation.

Getting ready for various stages of development and ongoing changes in how responses work

Seeing how little people change over time is one of the best things about being a parent or childcare worker. A gentle smile or a quiet word of approval worked great with my five-year-old Lia, but it was not as helpful when she was fifteen and trying to deal with social pressures, school, and finding her own identity. As parents, we must be flexible all the time because we know that as kids grow, they change how they ask for attention and say what they need.

As kids get older, their needs always change. As babies get older, they may not cry as much to get attention. By the time they are teenagers, they may use more complex behaviors like sulking, fighting, or isolating themselves to show that they need attention (Laursen & Collins, 2009). As parents, we need to change along with our kids.

Take Josh, my youngest child. As a baby, he was noticeably clear about what he wanted: hugs, to show me his newest block tower, or just to be carried around the house while I walked. He wants my attention less because he wants to be close to me and more because he wants to feel reassured or validated in more subtle ways, like when he asks for help with his science projects or quietly asks me to come to one of his school events. Now, the recognition he wants is confirmation that he is making progress as an adult.

As parents, we must adjust to this change by knowing how attention-seeking changes from someone who needs us to someone who wants to prove their independence. I also tell parents that when their kids' behaviors change, they should think about whether their reaction needs to change too. It is okay if the ways we learn to deal with emotional outbursts this year do not work next year. Being flexible is part of being a parent.

I remember a patient named Emily. She was nine years old, but her temper tantrums seemed like they came from a much younger kid.

Her parents said that all the usual advice for dealing with temper tantrums did not seem to work for her age. Through therapy, we learned that Emily was worried about her friends and school, and her outbursts, which seemed "immature," were signs of deeper, more complicated fears. We helped Emily's parents change how they responded to her behavior, going from punishing her to being more initiative-taking and open with her. This created a safe space for her to talk about her fears without having full-on meltdowns. Emily needed a different kind of attention—not the kind that fills in the gaps for younger kids, but attention that focused on including her in conversations about her worries and fears as she moved into pre-adolescence.

To sum up, if we want to successfully deal with attention-seeking behaviors, we need to be ready for ongoing changes:

- For babies and toddlers, give them instant comfort and safety.
- When the child is young, set clear limits and use positive feedback.
- When they are in school, talk back and forth, accept their independence, and help them learn how to solve problems.
- Focus on confirming who you are, fixing problems in a healthy way, and giving yourself time and space to be independent during pre-adolescence and adolescence.

As our kids grow up, they will get better at changing how they try to get our attention. We build confidence, emotional growth, and lifelong resilience by adapting our responses to their needs all the time (Lerner & Steinberg, 2009).

Why making a space with love, trust, clear expectations, and communication is so important.

Every parent wants to have a good bond with their child, one based on trust, love, and honest talk. To reach this goal, the setting we make at home is especially important. I often think about how my five kids, who all have different personalities, interacted with each other and how my wife and I worked to be consistent while still recognizing each child's uniqueness. To keep your child's attention-seeking behaviors from becoming a problem or becoming a part of their growth, it is important to create an environment of love, unconditional support, and clear expectations.

Trust and love go together. Maya has always been on the edge of what was possible because she is so lively and determined. But when my wife and I yearly met our obligations, I noticed something important: Maya was not pushing those limits to rebel; she was seeing if we were sticking to them. She felt safe within the limits we set because our answers were always the same: firm but fair. She knew she could trust the rules of the house and that love, and support would always be there for her, even when she acted out.

A boy named Max was a patient who helped me remember this lesson again. Max did not have any problems in school, but at home he was always acting out to get attention and was always evaluating his parents' limits and bounds. After collaborating with his parents, we found that they were missing an important part of being parents: discipline. Max did not know what would happen because family rules and responses seemed to change depending on how stressed out his parents were. Making outcomes clear and consistent was the key to finding a solution. It was also important to talk about why the limits were set in the first place.

It is not enough to have rules; our kids need to know why those rules are in place—to keep them safe physically and mentally, to teach them to be kind, and to teach them to be responsible. By setting clear goals and standards and being clear with Max, his behavior got better as he felt safer with the emotional boundaries at home.

A setting with a good balance of love, trust, clear standards, and open lines of communication is good for emotional growth. When these things are in place, kids feel safe to explore within safe, predictable limits. This makes them less likely to act out in unhealthy ways to get attention and helps parents and kids feel closer and safer together (Porges & Dana, 2018).

Attention-seeking can be turned into secure attachment and emotional growth. This is good news for parents and caregivers.

When I think about my time as a pediatrician and as a dad, I am profoundly moved by how things change when parents and other adults in charge take the time to change how they see attention-seeking. What may seem like times of anger or disagreement at first can turn into some of the most important chances for growth, for both you and your child.

I am proud of how Lia went from being a happy, curious kid to a strong, independent adult, or how Ethan went from being a boy who tried to get attention to a medical student who works hard to find his own way. They did want attention. But the attention they were looking for was not to compete, annoy, or cause trouble. It was a call to connect, a sign that they needed support, and an acknowledgement of how they were growing as people.

I have sat with a lot of parents who are dealing with attention-seeking behaviors—mothers crying in the emergency room, dads who are too busy and just need a break—and I have told them over and over, "You've got this." Remember that your child's attention-seeking is a way for them to say, "I need you," and how you react sets the tone for their emotional growth.

That is when we change: when we face these times with understanding, love, and trust. The tie gets stronger not because of perfect parenting but because of regular learning and respect for each other. We build strong bonds that will last a lifetime as we change our strategies and adapt to various times of life.

The most important thing for parents and caregivers to remember is that they do not have to give perfect answers all the time. The important thing is to make a space full of love, clear standards, and chances to talk to each other. You can turn times of anger into long-lasting, important connections with your child that will give them strength long after they no longer need your attention.

Finally, keep in mind that being a parent is an ongoing process. Each child, each stage of growth, and every new task are chances to learn, change, and grow together.

References

Calkins, S. D., & Leerkes, E. M. (2011). *Early attachment processes and the development of emotional self-regulation.* In K. D. Vohs & R. F. Baumeister (Eds.), Handbook of self-regulation: Research, theory, and applications (pp. 355–373). The Guilford Press.

Laursen, B., & Collins, W. A. (2009). *Parent-child relationships during adolescence.* In R. M. Lerner & L. Steinberg (Eds.), Handbook of adolescent psychology (Vol. 2, pp. 3-42). Wiley.

Lerner, R. M., & Steinberg, L. (Eds.). (2009). *Handbook of adolescent psychology: Contextual influences on adolescent development* (3rd ed.). Wiley.

Porges, S. W., & Dana, D. A. (2018). *The polyvagal theory in therapy: Engaging the rhythm of regulation.* Norton & Company.

Jordan R. Chavez IV, M.D.

Epilogue

When I think about all the years I have spent as a doctor, a pediatrician, and, most importantly, a dad to five kids, I feel incredibly thankful. Authoring this book has been both a way for me to think about myself and a way for me to share lessons with you, my friends. My kids—Lia, Ethan, Elai, Maya, and Josh—have taught me just as much, if not more, about how to connect with others, get attention, and grow emotionally than the 20 years I spent working in the emergency room.

What began as a question—why do kids act out to get attention? — grew into a deep respect for how complicated human growth is. I now understand that kids' attention-seeking habits are just a way for them to meet new people, feel accepted, and be noticed. Whether Ethan was dumping his Legos on the floor to get my attention away from my work or young Maya, the patient who wanted to relax after a long school day, these actions were less about getting in the way and more about a deep need to be seen, understood, and loved.

The things I have learned as a parent through years of practice and trial and error have led me to a simple truth: caring for, parenting, and guiding kids through their exciting, curious, and sometimes tough times of growth is all about building relationships. It means realizing that every cry, temper tantrum, interruption, or sulk has a need that needs to be met. How we manage these situations says a lot about who we are as parents and what kind of people our kids will become.

The title of this book is based on actions that try to get attention, since that is where a lot of the confusion starts. We often see these actions through a view that is clouded by stress, anger, or even overwhelm. Now that I've thought about it, the times when my patience as a doctor and as a parent was tried, I see that they were also chances—chances to connect with my kids, to hear what they weren't saying, and to help them become more emotionally strong.

I am telling you this not because I know everything (trust me, I do not), but because I have seen personally how things can change when we stop trying to control behavior and start making connections.

The Never-Ending Path of Growth—For Kids and Parents

Lia, my oldest daughter, just graduated from college. She is full of the freedom and confidence that we worked so hard to build in her as a child. Ethan is slowly learning how to be a doctor, which is a career he feels called to follow like I do. Elai, who likes to think things through, is deeply involved in his biology studies. Maya is making progress in her business major and making her own way. She is a very free-spirited person. And Josh, my youngest son, is well on his way to finishing his Medical Biology classes. He will become a doctor like his siblings.

However, as I write this conclusion, I cannot help but think that every day I and they are both growing emotionally. People still come to me for help, advice, and to connect with me. As they have grown up, their attempts to get attention have changed, but at their core, they still want to be heard, have their worth seen, and have their feelings accepted.

As parents and caregivers, we sometimes think that the "hard stuff" only happens when kids are kids and that things get easier after the tantrums and the teen years are over. That is not entirely true. What I have learned is that if our kids need someone to talk to, we will always be there for them as they build their mental health. When our kids are five or twenty-five, when they have a scraped knee or a broken heart, they will always need us to be there for them, to understand, and to tell them that we will always "see" them.

Parent after parent has asked me, "Does it ever get easier?" The answer is both yes and no. Things change. The problems take different forms, but they are still the same in heart. It is not our job to fix everything. It is to lead with understanding, set limits with kindness, and show others how to be emotionally strong. As parents, it is our job to be there for our kids as they learn, stumble, and find their way. We should always remember that their worth does not rest on how well they behave or how calm they stay, but on who they are as people who are learning how to deal with the complicated things in life.

One last word of encouragement

Just before I end this book, I want you to feel like you understand your child and yourself better. Not every parent is great. As a guardian, you do not know everything. This is a great trip where we are all learning together.

ATTENTION-SEEKING BEHAVIORS in CHILDREN

I have spent a lot of time in the clinical world making diagnoses, looking at symptoms, and coming to opinions. But being a parent has been different. It is more strange and bigger. The question does not just ask for smarts; it also asks for an open heart. By observing attention-seeking habits, I have learned that it is not about fixing or correcting them, but about becoming more aware of who our children are and what they need.

When your child wants your attention, it is a chance to get closer to them, build trust, and let them know that you love and value them no matter what. It is during times of trouble that relationships can grow the strongest.

Take heart, all of you parents, caregivers, teachers, and doctors reading these last few words. There are many interesting things about kids, but sometimes they will make us mad. They are giving us the chance to grow with them, though. They do not want to bother us; they need our help to understand the world, which might also help us understand ourselves a little better.

Be patient, stay interested, and most of all, stay linked. The best thing you can give is your presence—your real, caring, and understanding presence. It will affect how your kids see themselves, others, and the connections they make in the future.

In the end, having kids is not just about making them into the people they will become; it is also about making us into the people we will become while we patiently, humbly, and unconditionally love them through life.

Thanks for giving me the chance to share these thoughts, stories, and views. I hope that by reading them, you have felt better, been inspired, and even seen some parts of your own parenting story in them.

Enjoy the journey of growth, both for you and your child.

Jordan R. Chavez IV, M.D.

Onward, With Love and Grace.
Sincerely,

JORDAN R. CHAVEZ IV
Proud Father, Pediatrician, and Student of Life and Parenting

About the Author

Dr. Jordan R. Chavez IV is a distinguished physician from the Philippines with an impressive 24 years in medical practice, including 18 years dedicated to pediatrics and extensive experience in emergency medicine. His deep commitment to children's health and expertise in handling critical situations have made him a respected figure in his field.

Dr. Chavez holds a master's degree in hospital administration, which complements his clinical experience by providing him with insights into effective healthcare management. He is pursuing PhD studies in business management with a focus on international healthcare systems, reflecting his passion for improving healthcare delivery locally and globally. A devoted father of five, Dr. Chavez's family includes a college graduate in tourism as the eldest child; a second child who is currently studying medicine; a third pursuing biology with aspirations for medical school; a fourth studying finance; and the youngest also preparing for medical school through his studies in medical biology.

In addition to his clinical work and academic pursuits, Dr. Chavez has developed a keen interest in writing books to educate parents, relatives of patients, and patients about health and mental health issues. He believes that many illnesses stem from misunderstandings regarding various factors contributing to health problems, making it essential to promote preventive measures through education.

Through his writing and practice, Dr. Chavez inspires those around him while advocating for informed decision-making regarding healthcare with families and communities.

Printed in Great Britain
by Amazon